Rocal's Gastronomic Tariff

A Journey Through the Flavors, Traditions, and Regional Diversity of Rocal's Gastronomy

Table of Contents

Introduction 1

Chapter 1 The Roots of Rocal Cuisine 3

    Influences from Neighboring Regions 4

    Ancient Techniques and Modern Twists 5

    The Role of Agriculture in Flavor Development 6

Chapter 2 Signature Dishes of Rocal 9

    The Must-Try Comfort Foods 10

    Festive Feasts: Rocal's Special Occasion Meals 11

    Street Food: Savory Bites from the Heart of the City 12

Chapter 3 Flavors of the Land, Vegetables and Herbs 14

    Rocal's Garden Bounty 15

    The Medicinal and Flavorful Herbs 16

    Seasonal Vegetables in Traditional Dishes 17

Chapter 4 Meat and Poultry: A Carnivore's Paradise 19

    Pastoral Perfection: Cattle and Lamb 20

    Free-Range Birds: Poultry's Role in Rocal Kitchens 21

    Cooking with Game: Unique Flavors from the Wild 22

Chapter 5 Seafood and Waterways: The Bounty of Rocal's Shores 24

Freshwater Treasures: River and Lake Fish 25

Coastal Specialties: Rocal's Saltwater Delights........................ 26

Techniques for Perfecting Seafood Dishes................................ 27

Chapter 6 Desserts and Sweets: Rocal's Sweet Tooth 29

Traditional Pastries and Confections 30

Exotic Fruits in Rocal Desserts... 31

Sweets for the Soul: How Rocal Celebrates with Sugar............ 32

Chapter 7 Beverages of Rocal 34

The Rocal Brewing Tradition 35

Traditional Herbal Teas and Infusions 38

Alcoholic Delights: From Wine to Spirits 40

Chapter 8 The Art of Rocal Dining.. 43

The Role of Presentation in Rocal Cuisine................................ 44

Dining Etiquette: From Family Meals to Grand Gatherings 46

The Importance of Hospitality in Rocal Culture 48

Chapter 9 Cooking Techniques: From the Kitchen to the Table 51

Ancient Methods Still in Use.. 53

Modern Appliances Meet Traditional Recipes.......................... 55

Rocal's Approach to Preserving Flavor 57

Chapter 10 Rocal Cuisine in the Modern World 60

Fusion and Innovation in the Rocal Kitchen 62

The Global Influence of Rocal Dishes 64

The Future of Rocal Gastronomy 67

Chapter 11 Regional Variations: Exploring Rocal's Diversity 69

North vs South: Culinary Differences in Rocal.......................... 71

The Impact of Geography on Rocal Cuisine 74

How Local Ingredients Shape Regional Dishes 77

Chapter 12 The Cultural Significance of Food in Rocal...... 80

Food as a Reflection of Identity 82

Celebrations and Rituals: The Role of Food in Rocal Traditions 84

How Rocal Food Brings People Together.................................... 86

Conclusion 89

A Taste of Rocal: Why You Should Try These Recipes 90

Preserving the Tradition for Future Generations 92

Cooking as a Cultural Expression 95

Introduction

Rocal cuisine is a vibrant tapestry woven from centuries of cultural exchange, regional diversity, and culinary innovation. At its core, Rocal food represents the essence of its people, their history, and the land they cultivate. The culinary landscape of Rocal is not just a reflection of local ingredients but an embodiment of a rich tradition that blends ancient practices with modern influences. From the fields that nourish the crops to the kitchens where the magic happens, every dish tells a story of resilience, creativity, and passion.

The origins of Rocal's culinary practices can be traced back to ancient times, when the first settlers of this region began experimenting with the natural bounty that surrounded them. Over time, the region's cuisine was shaped by numerous influences—trade routes brought spices, flavors, and cooking techniques from distant lands, while neighboring cultures contributed to the development of unique local ingredients and dishes. This blending of different traditions gave rise to a gastronomic identity that is distinctly Rocal, yet deeply interconnected with the wider world.

Rocal food is more than just sustenance; it is a celebration of life, community, and tradition. Meals in Rocal are shared with family and friends, often accompanied by stories, laughter, and joy. The dining table is where social connections are made, and the act of cooking is a form of expression, passed down through generations. In this land, food represents both the past and the future—a living heritage that continues to evolve while honoring its roots.

A culinary journey through Rocal is an exploration of flavors that range from bold and spicy to subtle and aromatic, all influenced by the region's diverse geography. From the coastal shores where fresh seafood reigns to the fertile lands that produce rich vegetables and grains, each region of Rocal offers its own distinctive tastes and textures. The ingredients, harvested from the earth and sea, are transformed into dishes that are as much about the experience as they are about the flavor.

As you embark on this journey through Rocal's culinary treasures, you will discover not only recipes but also the stories of the people who have cultivated these traditions for generations. From humble street food to grand feasts, Rocal cuisine is an invitation to taste the heart of the region—one dish at a time.

Chapter 1
The Roots of Rocal Cuisine

Rocal cuisine is a beautiful fusion of ancient traditions, external influences, and local agricultural richness, each element contributing to the unique flavor profile of the region. The roots of Rocal's culinary identity lie in a history that spans centuries, shaped by interactions with neighboring regions and the evolving needs and preferences of its people. The cuisine reflects a deep connection between the land, its people, and their cooking practices, which have been passed down through generations.

The foundation of Rocal cuisine is heavily influenced by its geographical position, which placed it at the crossroads of various trade routes. These routes brought an array of spices, herbs, and cooking techniques that have been embraced and adapted by Rocal chefs. From the aromatic spices of the East to the rich influences of Mediterranean and African cuisines, Rocal food has evolved through a melting pot of global flavors, yet remains distinctively tied to its local agricultural traditions.

Ancient cooking techniques are an integral part of Rocal's culinary story. Traditional methods such as slow roasting, braising, and grilling over open flames have been refined over centuries.

These techniques emphasize the natural flavors of the ingredients, allowing the food to speak for itself. Although Rocal chefs respect these time-honored methods, they also embrace modern culinary techniques, blending the best of both worlds. The marriage of ancient traditions with contemporary innovations has helped keep Rocal cuisine both rooted in its history and dynamic in its evolution.

Agriculture has always played a crucial role in shaping Rocal's food culture. The fertile soil and diverse climate provide a bounty of ingredients that are central to Rocal dishes. From fresh vegetables and grains to the rich and varied meats, the agricultural landscape of Rocal ensures that its culinary traditions remain firmly connected to the earth. This chapter delves into the origins of Rocal cuisine, exploring how geography, history, and agriculture have converged to create a food culture like no other.

Influences from Neighboring Regions

Rocal's cuisine has evolved through centuries of interaction with neighboring cultures and regions. Its strategic location at the crossroads of important trade routes has made it a melting pot of culinary influences. Traders, explorers, and neighboring civilizations introduced spices, herbs, and cooking techniques that shaped Rocal's unique food culture. From the rich spices of the Middle East to the aromatic flavors of Asia and the Mediterranean, Rocal's culinary history is a reflection of these external exchanges.

One of the most significant influences comes from the East, where spices like cumin, cinnamon, and turmeric made their way into Rocal kitchens, adding warmth and complexity to dishes. These spices are now staples in many Rocal dishes, giving them a distinctive flavor profile. Additionally, the Mediterranean influence is evident in the use of olive oil, citrus fruits, and fresh herbs, which are used in cooking and garnishing a wide range of dishes. This combination of Eastern and Mediterranean ingredients brings a vibrant and aromatic character to Rocal's food.

Africa, too, played a vital role in shaping Rocal cuisine, particularly with the introduction of grains like millet, sorghum, and teff. These grains, now integrated into everyday meals, provide a nutritious base for many Rocal dishes. The influence of African cooking techniques, such as slow-cooking meats and stews, can also be traced in many Rocal recipes, which emphasize tender, flavorful meat and vegetable combinations.

Rocal cuisine's openness to these external influences is what makes it so diverse and dynamic. The way these global elements have been incorporated into local culinary practices has created a food culture that is not only unique to Rocal but also interconnected with the wider world.

Ancient Techniques and Modern Twists

Rocal's cuisine is grounded in ancient cooking methods that have been perfected over centuries. These time-honored techniques have been passed down through generations, each adding its own layer of refinement to the culinary tradition. From roasting meats over open flames to slow-braising stews in clay pots, these traditional practices emphasize simplicity, patience, and respect for the ingredients. Ancient methods allow the natural flavors of the food to shine through, creating dishes that are rich in taste and steeped in history.

Slow cooking, in particular, holds a special place in Rocal cuisine. Stews and soups simmer for hours, allowing the flavors to meld and intensify. This method is often used for tough cuts of meat, transforming them into tender, succulent dishes. Braising, which involves cooking meat in liquid at a low temperature, is another ancient technique that is commonly used in Rocal kitchens. This method, combined with herbs and spices, imparts a deep, savory flavor that is characteristic of Rocal dishes.

Grilling is another ancient cooking method that remains central to Rocal cuisine. Whether it's cooking skewers of marinated lamb or fish over an open flame, grilling imparts a smoky flavor that complements the rich spices and ingredients used in Rocal food. This method has been refined over the years, with modern tools like charcoal grills enhancing the cooking experience.

However, Rocal chefs are not bound by tradition alone. While they honor the ancient methods, they also embrace modern techniques and innovations. The introduction of modern appliances, such as pressure cookers and sous-vide machines, has allowed Rocal chefs to experiment with new textures and flavors, creating dishes that are both traditional and contemporary. These modern twists breathe new life into the cuisine, preserving the essence of ancient techniques while adapting to the fast-paced world of today's culinary landscape.

The Role of Agriculture in Flavor Development

Agriculture plays a pivotal role in the development of Rocal cuisine, providing the foundation for its rich and diverse flavors. The region's fertile land, coupled with a favorable climate, allows for the cultivation of a wide variety of crops that are essential to Rocal cooking. From vibrant vegetables and fresh fruits to hearty grains and aromatic herbs, the agricultural bounty of Rocal is integral to the flavors that define its cuisine.

The relationship between Rocal's agricultural practices and its cuisine is a symbiotic one. Local farmers understand the unique needs of the land and cultivate crops that thrive in the region's diverse microclimates. This deep connection to the land results in ingredients that are incredibly fresh, flavorful, and of the highest quality. Whether it's the tang of ripe tomatoes, the sweetness of locally grown melons, or the fragrance of fresh basil, the quality of these ingredients is evident in every dish.

The diversity of Rocal's agriculture is reflected in its cuisine, where a variety of grains, legumes, and vegetables are used in different combinations. For example, wheat and barley are staples in many Rocal dishes, providing the base for hearty breads and grains that complement stews and meats. The use of legumes such as lentils and chickpeas adds texture and richness to many traditional dishes, making them not only flavorful but also highly nutritious.

Herbs also play a significant role in flavor development. Rocal farmers cultivate a wide range of aromatic herbs, such as mint, rosemary, thyme, and oregano, which are used to season dishes and add layers of fragrance. These herbs are often grown in herb gardens close to homes and restaurants, ensuring that they are always fresh and available. The use of these local herbs adds a distinctively fresh and vibrant taste to Rocal food, enhancing the natural flavors of the ingredients.

Overall, the agricultural heritage of Rocal is at the heart of its cuisine. The region's commitment to preserving traditional farming methods, combined with modern sustainable practices, ensures that the flavors of Rocal will continue to thrive for generations to come.

Chapter 2
Signature Dishes of Rocal

The culinary landscape of Rocal is defined by its iconic dishes, each one telling the story of the region's culture, history, and community. From the comforting meals shared at family tables to the festive feasts enjoyed during celebrations, Rocal's signature dishes have become synonymous with the region's identity. These meals are more than just food; they are expressions of the warmth and hospitality that define Rocal's culinary heritage. In every bite, there's a connection to the land, the people, and the deep-rooted traditions that have been passed down through generations.

Comfort foods occupy a special place in Rocal's heart. These dishes, often rich in flavors and textures, provide a sense of home and nostalgia. Whether enjoyed on a rainy day or as part of a Sunday family gathering, these meals evoke a feeling of warmth and security. From slow-cooked stews to hearty grain-based dishes, comfort foods in Rocal are all about indulgence, simplicity, and satisfying the soul.

Festivals and special occasions in Rocal are marked by grand feasts, where families and communities come together to celebrate with food. These meals are often elaborate, featuring multiple courses and showcasing the best of Rocal's culinary craftsmanship. They are prepared with care and love, reflecting the joy and significance of the occasion. Whether it's a wedding, religious holiday, or harvest celebration, Rocal's special occasion meals are a highlight, bringing people together to share in both the flavors and the festivities.

On the streets of Rocal's bustling cities, vendors offer an entirely different type of dining experience. Street food, often quick and affordable, is a window into the everyday life of the region. These savory bites capture the essence of Rocal's vibrant food culture, offering a taste of authenticity in every dish. From grilled skewers to savory pastries, street food in Rocal is as much about convenience as it is about flavor and tradition.

The Must-Try Comfort Foods

Rocal's comfort foods are the soul of the region's culinary culture. These dishes, often enjoyed during moments of relaxation or when gathering with loved ones, embody warmth, tradition, and familiarity. At the heart of Rocal's comfort food scene are stews and slow-cooked dishes that fill the air with rich aromas and create an atmosphere of home. One of the most popular comfort foods is Rocal Stew, a slow-cooked combination of meats, vegetables, and hearty grains that simmer for hours, allowing the flavors to blend and intensify. This dish, often served with crusty bread or a side of rice, is a staple in many households and is associated with family gatherings.

Another must-try comfort food is Grilled Lamb Skewers, marinated in a mixture of local herbs, spices, and olive oil. These skewers are perfectly charred over an open flame, creating a smoky aroma that is both inviting and comforting. Served with a side of fresh vegetables or a yogurt-based sauce, they bring a touch of indulgence to everyday meals.

For those with a sweet tooth, Rocal Rice Pudding is a beloved dessert that provides both comfort and nostalgia. Made with milk, sugar, and a hint of vanilla, this dish is served warm or chilled and topped with cinnamon or nuts. It's the kind of dessert that transports people back to childhood, evoking memories of family meals and special occasions.

Rocal comfort foods offer a simple yet satisfying taste of the region's heart and history. These dishes are rich, filling, and deeply connected to the people who have passed down the recipes for generations, making them an essential part of any Rocal dining experience.

Festive Feasts: Rocal's Special Occasion Meals

Rocal's special occasion meals are an integral part of its cultural fabric, representing the region's appreciation for celebration, family, and food. These feasts are typically elaborate, often featuring multiple courses that showcase the culinary expertise and rich flavors of Rocal cuisine. They are served during festivals, weddings, religious holidays, and significant family milestones, marking these events with grandeur and joy.

One of the most iconic special occasion dishes is Rocal Lamb Pilaf, a fragrant rice dish cooked with tender, slow-braised lamb, seasoned with a blend of local spices such as cinnamon, cloves, and cardamom. The rice is cooked to perfection, absorbing the rich flavors of the meat and spices. This dish is often served alongside a vibrant vegetable salad, providing a refreshing contrast to the richness of the pilaf.

Another beloved festive meal is Stuffed Roasted Chicken, a whole bird stuffed with a mixture of grains, nuts, and dried fruits, creating a perfect balance of savory and sweet flavors. Roasted to golden perfection, this dish is the centerpiece of many family gatherings and is often accompanied by a tangy, spiced gravy that enhances its flavor.

For dessert, Rocal Baklava is a must-try during special occasions. Made with layers of thin pastry, chopped nuts, and honey syrup, this sweet treat is rich, sticky, and utterly indulgent. It's often served with a cup of strong, fragrant tea, adding a sense of ritual to the meal.

These special occasion meals are more than just food—they are a celebration of life, a reflection of Rocal's rich history, and a way for people to come together in joy and unity. The preparation and sharing of these dishes signify the importance of family, tradition, and community in Rocal culture.

Street Food: Savory Bites from the Heart of the City

Rocal's street food scene offers a dynamic and flavorful glimpse into the region's daily life. The streets are lined with vendors offering savory bites that are both quick and satisfying, representing the essence of Rocal's fast-paced yet culinary-rich lifestyle. From bustling markets to street corners, these small yet flavorful dishes capture the authenticity and vibrancy of the region's food culture.

One of the most popular street food items is Rocal Samosas, crispy triangular pastries filled with a spiced mixture of vegetables or minced meat. These golden pockets of deliciousness are fried to perfection and often served with a tangy tamarind chutney or a cooling yogurt dip. The crunchy exterior and flavorful filling make them a perfect on-the-go snack for those exploring the city.

Grilled Vegetable Skewers are another street food favorite, showcasing the region's abundant harvest of fresh vegetables. Zucchini, eggplant, and peppers are skewered and grilled over hot coals, often brushed with a simple marinade of olive oil, garlic, and herbs. The result is a smoky, tender bite of vegetables that highlights the fresh, seasonal ingredients of the region.

For a heartier snack, Rocal Flatbread with Lamb Filling is a street food staple that never disappoints. The soft, warm flatbread is stuffed with seasoned minced lamb, then grilled or baked to perfection. The juicy filling is complemented by a variety of toppings, including pickled vegetables, herbs, and a drizzle of spicy sauce. This dish is a satisfying meal on the go, offering a taste of Rocal's deep-rooted culinary traditions in a portable format.

Rocal's street food scene is an integral part of the city's cultural fabric, offering a delicious and accessible way for locals and visitors alike to experience the bold, diverse flavors of the region in their most authentic form. Each bite of these savory street foods offers a taste of Rocal's rich culinary heritage, providing a delicious snapshot of the region's daily life and flavors.

Chapter 3
Flavors of the Land, Vegetables and Herbs

Rocal's cuisine is deeply rooted in the land, and nowhere is this more evident than in the region's vegetables and herbs. The fertile soil and diverse climate of Rocal provide an abundance of fresh produce that is central to its culinary identity. From vibrant, leafy greens to aromatic herbs, the region's vegetables and herbs not only add flavor but also reflect the agricultural heritage of the area. These ingredients, often grown locally by farmers with deep knowledge of the land, play an essential role in defining the taste of Rocal's dishes.

Vegetables in Rocal are much more than just accompaniments; they are the heart of many meals, adding depth, texture, and a burst of natural flavor to every dish. Root vegetables, such as carrots and beets, are staples in soups and stews, their earthy sweetness enriching the broth. Leafy greens like spinach and kale are often featured in salads and sautéed dishes, providing a fresh, vibrant contrast to richer, meat-heavy meals. The region's abundant tomatoes, peppers, and cucumbers are essential in both raw and cooked preparations, lending their bright, tangy flavors to a variety of dishes.

Herbs are just as important as vegetables in Rocal cooking, and the local gardens are filled with an array of aromatic plants. Mint, cilantro, basil, and parsley are used generously to season both hot and cold dishes, enhancing the flavors with their fresh, fragrant notes. These herbs are often combined with spices to create complex and layered flavors, from tangy dips to refreshing salads. The emphasis on fresh herbs elevates every meal, turning simple ingredients into something truly special.

In this chapter, we will explore the diverse vegetables and herbs that define Rocal cuisine, showcasing how they bring balance, brightness, and authenticity to the region's vibrant food culture.

Rocal's Garden Bounty

Rocal's fertile soil and temperate climate make it an agricultural paradise, providing a diverse array of produce that forms the backbone of its cuisine. The region's gardens are filled with an abundance of fruits, vegetables, and herbs, each one carefully cultivated by local farmers who understand the nuances of the land. From rich, earthy root vegetables to tender, leafy greens, the bounty of Rocal's gardens plays a central role in shaping the flavors of its food.

Tomatoes, cucumbers, and peppers are some of the most common vegetables found in Rocal gardens. These vibrant and juicy ingredients are used in everything from fresh salads to tangy salsas, where their natural sweetness is balanced by the region's signature spices. Rocal's variety of leafy greens, such as spinach, kale, and arugula, adds both color and freshness to a wide range of dishes. These greens are often paired with hearty grains, grains, and meats, adding texture and nutritional value to the meal.

In addition to vegetables, Rocal's gardens also produce an array of fruits, including figs, melons, and citrus fruits. These fruits are often incorporated into savory dishes, adding a natural sweetness and acidity that enhances the overall flavor profile. Fruits are also used in desserts, where they are combined with spices and herbs to create a tantalizing contrast of flavors.

The abundance of produce grown in Rocal's gardens is not only a source of pride for the region but also a testament to the people's deep connection to the land. With each harvest, the land continues to provide the foundation for Rocal's culinary traditions, ensuring that its food culture remains rooted in the fertile soil that sustains it.

The Medicinal and Flavorful Herbs

Herbs are an essential component of Rocal cuisine, not only for their ability to elevate flavors but also for their rich medicinal properties. The region's herbs are carefully cultivated and harvested from the abundant gardens, offering a wide range of benefits that go beyond their culinary uses. These herbs, many of which have been used for centuries, bring both medicinal and aromatic qualities to the table, allowing Rocal's chefs to craft dishes that are as healing as they are flavorful.

Mint is one of the most widely used herbs in Rocal cooking. Known for its refreshing, cooling properties, mint is used in a variety of dishes, from salads to drinks, and even as a garnish for desserts. In Rocal culture, mint is not just a flavor enhancer; it is also valued for its digestive benefits and soothing qualities, making it an essential herb for promoting health.

Cilantro, with its bright, citrusy flavor, is another herb commonly found in Rocal kitchens. It is often used in chutneys, salads, and marinades, adding a fresh, aromatic element to the dish. Beyond its culinary uses, cilantro is also known for its detoxifying properties, aiding in digestion and promoting overall health. Parsley, thyme, and rosemary are also frequently used in Rocal cooking, each contributing a unique flavor profile while offering health benefits. Parsley is known for its high vitamin content and is often used in dishes that require a light, herbal touch, while thyme and rosemary are prized for their antimicrobial and anti-inflammatory properties.

The use of these medicinal herbs reflects Rocal's holistic approach to food, where the act of eating is not only about nourishment but also about enhancing well-being. The combination of flavor and function is what makes Rocal's use of herbs truly special, with each meal providing not just taste but health benefits as well.

Seasonal Vegetables in Traditional Dishes

Seasonal vegetables are at the heart of many traditional Rocal dishes, and their availability throughout the year determines the flavors and ingredients that dominate the culinary scene. Rocal cuisine places great importance on using fresh, in-season vegetables, as they are at their peak in flavor and nutritional value. The region's climate allows for the cultivation of a wide variety of vegetables that change with the seasons, creating a dynamic and ever-evolving food culture.

In the spring, tender greens like spinach and lettuce are featured prominently in Rocal dishes. These delicate vegetables are often used in fresh salads, where they are combined with bright citrus fruits and topped with a drizzle of olive oil. As the weather warms, zucchini and eggplant become key players in Rocal cooking, often grilled or roasted to bring out their natural sweetness and smoky flavor. These vegetables are also used in stews, where they absorb the rich spices and broths of the dish.

Summer brings an abundance of tomatoes, peppers, and cucumbers, which are used in refreshing salads and cooling salsas. These vegetables are often paired with herbs like basil and parsley, which are also in full bloom during the summer months. The combination of fresh vegetables and herbs creates dishes that are light, vibrant, and full of flavor.

As fall arrives, root vegetables like carrots, beets, and sweet potatoes come into their own. These hearty vegetables are used in soups, stews, and roasted dishes, where their earthy sweetness is balanced by savory ingredients. Fall also brings an abundance of squashes and pumpkins, which are used in both savory dishes and desserts, adding depth and richness to the meals.

By incorporating seasonal vegetables into traditional dishes, Rocal cuisine remains deeply connected to the rhythms of nature. The ever-changing availability of produce allows chefs to create meals that are always fresh, flavorful, and reflective of the season.

Chapter 4
Meat and Poultry: A Carnivore's Paradise

Meat and poultry hold a revered place in Rocal cuisine, where the rich flavors and textures of animal proteins are celebrated in a variety of traditional dishes. Rocal's diverse culinary culture has been shaped by the abundance of high-quality meat, sourced from local livestock and poultry, which are raised in the region's fertile pastures and farms. The combination of exceptional ingredients and time-honored cooking methods has made meat and poultry an essential component of Rocal's gastronomic identity.

Rocal's relationship with meat goes beyond mere sustenance—it's a reflection of cultural values, hospitality, and community. Meat is often reserved for special occasions, family gatherings, and festivals, where it is prepared with great care and shared with loved ones. Whether it's slow-braising lamb in rich spices or grilling tender cuts of beef over an open flame, Rocal's approach to cooking meat is about more than just satisfying hunger; it's about creating an experience that brings people together around the table.

Lamb, beef, and poultry are the cornerstones of Rocal's meat offerings. The region's lamb is particularly prized for its tenderness and rich flavor, making it a key ingredient in stews, roasts, and skewers. Beef, often marinated in a blend of herbs and spices, is enjoyed in a variety of forms, from juicy steaks to flavorful stews. Poultry, including chicken and duck, is prepared in many different ways, ranging from slow-cooked dishes to crispy, roasted specialties.

In this chapter, we will explore the world of Rocal's meats and poultry, examining the dishes that showcase these ingredients in their full glory. From humble preparations to grand feasts, meat and poultry are at the heart of Rocal's culinary tradition, providing both flavor and a sense of connection to the land and its people.

Pastoral Perfection: Cattle and Lamb

In Rocal cuisine, cattle and lamb hold a special place of honor, with their meat forming the foundation of many traditional dishes. The region's pastoral landscape, with its lush pastures and fertile grasslands, provides the perfect environment for raising cattle and sheep, which thrive on the natural, high-quality grasses found in the area. The animals are known for their tenderness and rich flavor, which is a direct result of their diet and the care with which they are raised.

Rocal's beef and lamb are often the centerpiece of large family meals and festive occasions, prepared in a variety of ways that highlight their deep, savory flavors. Slow-cooking methods, such as braising and stewing, are common in Rocal kitchens, allowing the meats to absorb the aromatic spices and herbs with which they are paired. For example, Rocal Lamb Stew, made with tender cuts of lamb, garlic, rosemary, and root vegetables, is a dish that epitomizes the richness of pastoral meat. The slow-cooking process renders the meat meltingly tender, allowing the deep flavors of the lamb to come through, creating a comforting, hearty dish.

Grilled meats also have a significant presence in Rocal cuisine. Cuts of beef and lamb are marinated in a variety of local herbs and spices before being grilled over an open flame, giving the meat a smoky, charred exterior and a juicy, flavorful interior. Rocal BBQ Lamb, with its aromatic blend of garlic, olive oil, and cumin, is a popular dish at gatherings and celebrations, showcasing the simplicity and perfection of cooking with high-quality meat.

The emphasis on pastoral perfection in Rocal cuisine reflects a deep respect for the land and animals that provide sustenance, with each dish celebrating the natural flavors that come from responsibly raised cattle and lamb.

Free-Range Birds: Poultry's Role in Rocal Kitchens

Poultry is a cornerstone of Rocal cuisine, valued for its versatility, tenderness, and ability to absorb a wide range of spices and flavors. Raised in free-range environments, the birds in Rocal are allowed to roam freely, foraging on natural grasses and seeds, which contributes to the distinct, rich flavor of the meat. This free-range practice results in poultry that is leaner, more flavorful, and healthier than conventionally farmed birds, making it an integral part of Rocal kitchens.

Chicken is the most commonly used poultry in Rocal dishes, appearing in countless preparations that showcase its ability to absorb both simple and complex flavor profiles. One of the most beloved dishes is Rocal Roast Chicken, where the bird is seasoned with a blend of fresh herbs, garlic, and citrus, then slow-roasted until golden and crisp. The tender, juicy meat, combined with the fragrant seasoning, creates a dish that is both comforting and aromatic, often served alongside roasted vegetables or a fresh salad.

Duck also plays an important role in Rocal cuisine, often prepared during special occasions and feasts. The rich, gamey flavor of duck pairs beautifully with fruit-based sauces, such as a tangy orange glaze or a sweet pomegranate reduction, creating a balance of savory and sweet flavors. Rocal Duck with Pomegranate Sauce is a dish that highlights the skill of Rocal chefs, using the natural sweetness of the fruit to complement the richness of the duck.

Poultry is also often featured in stews, curries, and soups, where it's slow-cooked to absorb the flavors of the broth and spices. Rocal Chicken Stew, made with root vegetables, herbs, and a variety of spices, is a hearty and flavorful dish enjoyed by many. The use of free-range poultry elevates these dishes, ensuring that every bite is tender, flavorful, and deeply satisfying.

Cooking with Game: Unique Flavors from the Wild

Game meat holds a special place in Rocal cuisine, offering a unique and flavorful alternative to traditional meats. The region's vast forests, hills, and wilderness areas are home to a wide variety of game animals, from wild boar and venison to rabbit and pheasant. These animals are hunted sustainably, with respect for nature, and their meat is prized for its rich, gamey flavor, which adds a distinct character to Rocal dishes.

One of the most celebrated game meats in Rocal kitchens is venison, known for its lean texture and deep, earthy taste. Rocal Venison Stew is a popular dish that highlights the natural richness of the meat. The venison is marinated in a blend of herbs and spices, then slow-cooked with root vegetables and red wine, resulting in a tender and flavorful stew. The earthy taste of the venison is complemented by the sweet undertones of the vegetables and the acidity of the wine, creating a dish that is both hearty and sophisticated.

Wild boar is another sought-after game meat in Rocal cuisine. Known for its robust, slightly sweet flavor, wild boar is often roasted or braised in a variety of dishes. Rocal Wild Boar with Herbs is a classic preparation, where the boar is seasoned with rosemary, garlic, and olive oil, then roasted until crispy on the outside and tender on the inside. The meat is often paired with wild mushrooms or a tangy fruit sauce to balance its richness.

Rocal also incorporates smaller game birds, such as pheasant and partridge, into its dishes. These birds are often roasted whole, served with a rich, flavorful gravy, or cooked in a fragrant herb-filled broth. Game birds bring a touch of rustic elegance to the table, their tender meat offering a delightful contrast to the bold, aromatic flavors that are common in Rocal cuisine.

Cooking with game allows Rocal chefs to explore the unique flavors of the wild, creating dishes that are deeply connected to the land and traditions of the region. Whether it's the tender richness of venison or the robust flavor of wild boar, game meat brings an exciting, adventurous element to the table, offering a taste of the wild in every bite.

Chapter 5
Seafood and Waterways: The Bounty of Rocal's Shores

The coastal region of Rocal is a haven for seafood lovers, with its pristine shores and bountiful waterways offering a wealth of fresh, high-quality fish and shellfish. The surrounding seas, rivers, and lakes are teeming with marine life, providing the region with an abundance of seafood that plays a central role in its culinary traditions. From salty sea breezes to crystal-clear waters, Rocal's geographical location ensures that its seafood is not only plentiful but also rich in flavor and diversity.

Seafood in Rocal is more than just a source of nourishment; it's a reflection of the region's deep connection to its waterways. Fishermen, who have passed their skills down through generations, navigate the local waters, harvesting fish and shellfish that are prized for their freshness and taste. Whether it's the delicate, flaky white fish found in the deep waters or the succulent shellfish harvested from the rocky coastline, Rocal's seafood is a testament to the purity and richness of the region's natural resources.

In Rocal kitchens, seafood is prepared in a variety of ways that highlight its natural flavors. Grilled fish, often seasoned with a simple rub of salt, olive oil, and lemon, is a popular choice, allowing the freshness of the catch to shine. Stews and soups, like the traditional Rocal Fish Chowder, are also common, where fish is combined with vegetables, herbs, and spices in a fragrant broth. The region's seafood is often paired with locally grown vegetables and aromatic herbs, creating dishes that are light, flavorful, and nourishing.

This chapter delves into the rich bounty of Rocal's shores, celebrating the variety and versatility of its seafood. Whether it's a simple grilled fish or a complex seafood stew, the ocean's bounty provides a delicious connection to the land, culture, and history of Rocal.

Freshwater Treasures: River and Lake Fish

Rocal's rivers and lakes are home to a variety of freshwater fish, each offering distinct flavors and textures that have become integral to the region's culinary traditions. These waters, rich in biodiversity, provide fish that are both flavorful and versatile, used in a range of dishes that showcase the pristine quality of the catch. From the tranquil rivers to the expansive lakes, the freshwater fish in Rocal are prized for their delicate, clean taste, making them a favorite ingredient in many traditional meals.

Among the most popular freshwater fish in Rocal are bass, perch, and trout. These fish are typically caught fresh and prepared in simple yet flavorful ways. Rocal Trout, often grilled or baked, is a dish that highlights the tender, flaky texture of the fish. Seasoned with a sprinkle of herbs and a squeeze of citrus, the trout is cooked to perfection, allowing its natural flavor to shine. The subtle sweetness of the fish pairs wonderfully with seasonal vegetables, making it a perfect dish for any occasion.

Rocal's river and lake fish are also used in hearty stews and soups. Rocal Fish Soup, made with a mix of freshwater fish, vegetables, and aromatic spices, is a popular dish that warms both the body and soul. The fish, slow-cooked in a fragrant broth, absorbs the rich flavors of the herbs and spices, resulting in a comforting and satisfying meal. The addition of fresh herbs like dill and parsley enhances the dish, adding a fresh, herbal note that balances the richness of the fish.

Freshwater fish in Rocal cuisine are not only an essential part of the local diet but also a symbol of the region's deep connection to its rivers and lakes, providing both sustenance and a taste of the land's natural bounty.

Coastal Specialties: Rocal's Saltwater Delights

The salty waters surrounding Rocal's coast are a treasure trove of marine life, offering an abundance of saltwater fish and shellfish that are integral to the region's rich culinary culture. The Rocal coastline, with its pristine beaches and rocky outcrops, is home to a variety of seafood that is both flavorful and abundant. The proximity to the ocean ensures that seafood is not only fresh but also prepared with a deep understanding of the delicate balance between the ocean and the kitchen.

Among Rocal's saltwater delights, fish like snapper, grouper, and mackerel are some of the most prized catches. These fish are known for their firm, meaty texture and are often prepared in simple yet flavorful ways. One popular preparation is Rocal Grilled

Snapper, where the fish is seasoned with a blend of herbs, garlic, and lemon, then grilled over an open flame. The result is a smoky, juicy fish that retains its natural sweetness, making it a favorite at seafood feasts and gatherings.

Shellfish, too, plays a vital role in Rocal's coastal cuisine. Shrimp, crabs, and clams are commonly used in a wide range of dishes, from seafood pastas to savory pies. Rocal Crab Cakes, made with tender crab meat, herbs, and breadcrumbs, are a beloved appetizer or main dish, often served with a tangy dipping sauce. The delicate sweetness of the crab is perfectly complemented by the seasoning, creating a flavorful, satisfying bite.

Rocal's coastal specialties celebrate the bounty of the sea, with each dish showcasing the fresh, flavorful seafood that has been harvested from the surrounding waters. Whether it's a perfectly grilled fish or a savory shellfish dish, the ocean's offerings are a central part of Rocal's culinary identity, bringing a taste of the sea to every meal.

Techniques for Perfecting Seafood Dishes

In Rocal, seafood is not just an ingredient but an art form, with chefs using a variety of time-tested techniques to bring out the best in every catch. The region's deep connection to the sea and its rich fishing heritage has given rise to a culinary tradition that emphasizes the delicate handling and preparation of seafood. From grilling to steaming and poaching, Rocal chefs employ a range of techniques that ensure the freshness and flavor of the seafood shine through in every dish.

One of the most common techniques used in Rocal kitchens is grilling. Grilling seafood, especially fish like snapper, bass, and mackerel, imparts a smoky flavor that enhances the natural taste of the fish. The key to perfect grilled seafood is to use the right heat and seasoning. Rocal chefs often season the fish with a simple blend of herbs, olive oil, and citrus, allowing the natural flavors of the fish to remain the star of the dish. The fish is grilled until just tender, ensuring that it remains juicy and flavorful without drying out.

Poaching is another popular technique for cooking seafood in Rocal. Poaching involves gently simmering fish in a flavorful liquid, such as broth, wine, or a citrus-based sauce. This technique is often used for delicate fish, such as trout and sole, as it preserves the fish's moisture and tenderness. The poaching liquid, often infused with herbs and spices, imparts subtle flavors to the fish, creating a light, aromatic dish that is both delicate and satisfying.

Steaming is a technique that is commonly used for shellfish, such as clams, mussels, and shrimp. The gentle heat of the steam ensures that the shellfish cook evenly and retain their natural juices. Steamed seafood is often served with a simple dip or sauce, such as garlic butter or a tangy tomato-based sauce, allowing the sweetness of the shellfish to shine through.

By combining these techniques with fresh, high-quality ingredients, Rocal chefs create seafood dishes that are both refined and full of flavor. Whether it's grilling, poaching, or steaming, each technique is designed to highlight the natural qualities of the seafood, ensuring that every bite is a celebration of the ocean's bounty.

Chapter 6
Desserts and Sweets: Rocal's Sweet Tooth

Rocal's culinary landscape is not only defined by its savory dishes but also by its irresistible array of desserts and sweets, which reflect the region's love for indulgence and celebration. The rich, diverse culture of Rocal extends to its sweet offerings, where a balance of flavors, textures, and traditional techniques come together to create desserts that are both comforting and delightful. Desserts in Rocal are not simply after-meal treats; they are woven into the fabric of everyday life, often served as a symbol of hospitality, joy, and the sweetness of shared moments.

A hallmark of Rocal sweets is their reliance on local ingredients that are abundant in the region, from luscious fruits to aromatic spices and rich dairy. Honey, sugar, nuts, and fruits like figs, dates, and citrus are frequently used to add natural sweetness and depth to the desserts, offering a flavor profile that is both indulgent and refreshing. Rocal desserts are often flavored with fragrant spices such as cinnamon, cardamom, and saffron, which elevate the simple sweetness of the dish and create an aromatic experience that tantalizes the senses.

Traditional desserts like Rocal Baklava, with its delicate layers of filo pastry, chopped nuts, and honey syrup, or Rice Pudding with Cinnamon, a creamy, comforting dessert flavored with vanilla and topped with a sprinkle of cinnamon, have long been family favorites. These sweets, often passed down through generations, are prepared with care and love, ensuring that each bite is a taste of Rocal's rich culinary heritage.

This chapter will explore the sweet side of Rocal, showcasing its most beloved desserts and sweets. From flaky pastries to rich puddings and fruit-based delicacies, Rocal's desserts are a testament to the region's love for all things sweet, offering a taste of happiness in every bite.

Traditional Pastries and Confections

Rocal's traditional pastries and confections are a delicious testament to the region's long-standing dessert culture, where sweets are not only enjoyed for their flavor but also for their connection to family, tradition, and celebration. The intricate craftsmanship behind these pastries reflects the region's deep appreciation for both fine technique and the joy of indulgence. Rocal bakers take immense pride in their craft, using time-honored recipes and fresh, local ingredients to create sweets that are as beautiful as they are flavorful.

One of the most iconic pastries in Rocal is Rocal Baklava, a delicate layered pastry made with thin sheets of filo dough, chopped nuts (usually pistachios or walnuts), and sweetened with honey or sugar syrup. The key to perfect baklava lies in the precise layering of the filo dough and the slow baking process, which results in a crisp, golden exterior that contrasts perfectly with the rich, nutty filling.

Often served as a dessert at family gatherings and celebrations, baklava is a beloved sweet that captures the essence of Rocal's pastry tradition.

Another popular confection is Rocal Ma'amoul, shortbread-like cookies filled with dates, figs, or nuts. These cookies are often made in intricate molds, giving them a distinctive appearance that adds a touch of elegance to any dessert table. The combination of the crumbly, buttery dough and the sweet, sticky filling creates a delightful balance of texture and flavor, making ma'amoul a favorite treat, particularly during festivals and holidays.

Traditional pastries like these are often accompanied by strong, aromatic tea or coffee, making them perfect for social gatherings. Their preparation requires a meticulous hand and an understanding of flavor balance, allowing these desserts to be passed down through generations and continue to hold a special place in Rocal's culinary heritage.

Exotic Fruits in Rocal Desserts

Rocal's diverse climate and fertile soils provide a bounty of exotic fruits that play a significant role in the region's dessert culture. These fruits, often bursting with flavor, lend a natural sweetness and a vibrant color to Rocal's sweet dishes. The use of fresh, seasonal fruits in desserts ensures that every bite is not only indulgent but also deeply connected to the land and the rhythms of nature.

One of the most beloved fruits in Rocal desserts is the Pomegranate. Known for its jewel-like seeds, pomegranate is used in a variety of sweet dishes, from syrups to fruit salads. Pomegranate Molasses, a sweet-tart reduction of the fruit's juice, is often drizzled over desserts like Rocal Rice Pudding or used as a glaze for cakes. The deep red color of the pomegranate gives a rich visual appeal to the desserts, while the tangy sweetness adds a refreshing contrast to heavier, richer elements like cream or honey.

Figs, both fresh and dried, are another key ingredient in Rocal desserts. Whether incorporated into pastries, jams, or eaten on their own, figs offer a natural sweetness and a soft, chewy texture that pairs perfectly with the region's nut-based sweets. Fig Tarts are a popular dessert where fresh figs are placed atop a buttery pastry crust and baked with a touch of honey and cinnamon, creating a perfect balance of sweetness and spice.

Exotic citrus fruits, like Rocal Oranges and Lemons, are also commonly used in desserts. Their bright, zesty flavor is often paired with delicate syrups and creams. Orange Blossom Panna Cotta is a popular dessert in Rocal, where the floral sweetness of the orange blossom is infused into a creamy custard base, offering a refreshing end to any meal. These fruits, both indigenous and cultivated, bring a touch of the wild into Rocal's sweet offerings, creating a vibrant and unique flavor profile that distinguishes Rocal desserts from those found in other parts of the world.

Sweets for the Soul: How Rocal Celebrates with Sugar

In Rocal, sweets are not just about indulgence—they are a vital part of the cultural fabric, used to celebrate life, family, and special occasions. The region's deep-rooted connection to food as a source of joy and community is reflected in the way desserts are enjoyed. Sugar, in all its forms, is the key ingredient in Rocal's most beloved sweets, symbolizing happiness, abundance, and the sweetness of life itself.

One of the most important aspects of Rocal's dessert culture is the role of sweets in marking celebrations. Birthdays, weddings, religious holidays, and local festivals are all occasions where desserts take center stage. The act of sharing sweets during these events goes beyond just eating; it's about bringing people together, offering hospitality, and celebrating the bonds of family and friendship. Rocal Halva, a semolina-based dessert sweetened with sugar and infused with rosewater or saffron, is often served during festive meals. Its rich, fragrant flavor and melt-in-the-mouth texture make it a perfect symbol of celebration and joy.

Rocal Baklava and Ma'amoul also serve as symbols of hospitality and tradition. These pastries are often made in large batches, and they're offered to guests as a way of welcoming them into the home. The intricate process of making these sweets — layering filo dough or carefully stuffing cookies with date paste — reflects the time and care taken in preparing food for loved ones, highlighting the importance of generosity and connection.

Desserts are also a means of honoring local customs and rituals. For instance, during Eid or other religious celebrations, families will come together to make Rocal Dates with Nuts, a simple yet profound sweet that represents the sharing of blessings. The act of preparing these sweets, often passed down through generations, connects people not just to their family but to the broader cultural history of Rocal. In this way, sweets are far more than just food — they are a vital part of the celebration of life, a means of nourishing the soul and the spirit of togetherness.

Chapter 7
Beverages of Rocal

Beverages in Rocal are more than just thirst-quenchers; they are an integral part of the region's culture, steeped in tradition and often associated with moments of hospitality, relaxation, and celebration. From the bustling street markets to family gatherings, Rocal's drinks are as diverse and flavorful as its cuisine, offering a refreshing contrast to the rich, savory dishes that define the culinary landscape. Whether it's a hot cup of fragrant tea or a chilled glass of freshly squeezed juice, beverages in Rocal are crafted with an emphasis on balance, taste, and the enjoyment of the moment.

At the heart of Rocal's beverage culture is Rocal Tea, a symbol of hospitality and community. Tea is enjoyed throughout the day, from early mornings to late evenings, and is often accompanied by a sweet pastry or light snack. The most popular varieties are infused with local herbs like mint and sage, creating a fragrant, soothing drink that is as much about ritual as it is about refreshment. The preparation and serving of tea in Rocal homes are done with great care, often shared among friends and family in a social setting, reflecting the importance of connection in Rocal society.

In addition to traditional teas, Rocal is known for its array of fruit-based beverages, often made with local, seasonal fruits. Freshly squeezed juices, such as pomegranate, orange, and apple, are common choices, providing a sweet, natural way to cool down in the warm climate. These juices are sometimes spiced with a hint of ginger or lemon, adding an extra layer of complexity to the flavors.

Alcoholic beverages also hold a place in Rocal's culinary traditions. Rocal Wine and Rocal Arak, a traditional anise-flavored spirit, are enjoyed during special occasions and celebrations, providing a rich, flavorful accompaniment to the region's savory and sweet dishes.

This chapter will explore the diverse range of beverages that define Rocal's culture, from the calming teas to the invigorating fruit juices and the celebratory spirits, all of which contribute to the region's rich, multifaceted culinary identity.

The Rocal Brewing Tradition

The art of brewing in Rocal is not just a culinary practice; it's an age-old tradition that has been passed down through generations. This brewing tradition involves more than just the production of beverages; it represents a deep connection to the land, the culture, and the people who have honed their craft over centuries. Brewing is embedded in Rocal's communal and social practices, with each brew carrying a story, a history, and an experience that is shared among family members, friends, and communities.

At the heart of the Rocal brewing tradition is Rocal Tea, a beverage that is more than just a drink; it is a daily ritual, a symbol of hospitality, and an essential part of the region's identity. Rocal tea is brewed from a variety of local herbs and leaves, each with its own distinctive flavor and health benefits. The most popular tea in Rocal is mint tea, a refreshing, aromatic beverage made from fresh mint leaves harvested from local gardens. This tea is typically brewed with boiling water, and sugar is added to taste, creating a balanced, soothing beverage. The deep cultural significance of mint tea in Rocal cannot be overstated—it is a beverage that signifies warmth, kindness, and the bond between those who share it.

Brewing in Rocal goes beyond just tea, however. Herbal infusions, made from locally foraged herbs, flowers, and roots, are an integral part of the region's brewing tradition. These infusions are believed to have medicinal properties, promoting relaxation, digestive health, and overall well-being. Common herbs used in Rocal brewing include chamomile, sage, thyme, and lavender. These herbs are carefully selected for their health benefits and are often blended to create calming, restorative teas. Rocal herbal infusions are a deeply comforting part of the cultural fabric, offering both nourishment and a connection to the land from which they originate.

In addition to herbal infusions, Rocal Coffee has gained prominence in recent decades as a beverage of choice for many. The coffee brewing process in Rocal is unique, often involving a slow drip method that allows the coffee grounds to steep for a longer period, creating a rich, intense flavor. Rocal coffee is typically served black, with minimal sugar, and is often accompanied by pastries or savory snacks. The preparation and serving of coffee are done with the same level of attention and care as traditional tea brewing, underscoring the importance of the brewing culture in Rocal's daily life.

Rocal's brewing tradition is not limited to hot beverages. Rocal Fruit Brews, such as fermented fruit teas and lightly alcoholic fruit-based drinks, are popular among locals, particularly during the warm months. These brews are made by fermenting seasonal fruits such as pomegranates, figs, or citrus fruits, and the result is a refreshing, lightly carbonated drink that is both sweet and tangy. These beverages are typically served chilled and are often enjoyed at festivals and gatherings, adding a celebratory touch to social occasions.

The brewing tradition in Rocal is rooted in the region's agricultural practices. Local farmers and artisans, often using age-old methods, cultivate the plants, fruits, and herbs used in these beverages. The ingredients are carefully selected for their quality, flavor, and health benefits, and many are grown organically, ensuring that each brew is as pure and natural as possible. Brewing in Rocal is both a science and an art, with each individual or family having their own unique recipes and techniques that have been passed down through generations.

In Rocal, brewing is not just about creating a beverage; it is about creating an experience. Whether it's a quiet moment of reflection with a hot cup of mint tea, a social gathering with friends sharing fruit brews, or a celebratory occasion marked by the richness of a perfectly brewed cup of coffee, the act of brewing is woven into the fabric of Rocal's social life and culture. It's a tradition that continues to evolve, but one that remains rooted in respect for the land, the craft, and the people who pass it on.

Traditional Herbal Teas and Infusions

Herbal teas and infusions have long been a cornerstone of Rocal's beverage culture, prized not only for their refreshing flavors but also for their medicinal and therapeutic properties. These infusions, often prepared using a combination of locally sourced herbs, flowers, and fruits, are woven into the daily lives of Rocal's people, providing comfort, relaxation, and a deep connection to the region's rich natural landscape. The tradition of brewing herbal teas is an age-old practice, passed down through generations, and remains an essential part of Rocal's culinary and cultural heritage.

The foundation of Rocal's herbal tea culture lies in the abundance of local plants and herbs that thrive in the region's diverse climate. Mint, chamomile, sage, thyme, and lavender are just a few of the many herbs that are commonly used to create infusions. These herbs are carefully chosen for their aromatic qualities and their ability to offer therapeutic benefits. For example, mint is known for its cooling, soothing properties, making it an ideal choice for relieving digestive issues and promoting relaxation. Chamomile, with its gentle, floral flavor, is often brewed to help with sleep and anxiety, while sage and thyme are used for their digestive and antimicrobial properties.

In addition to these common herbs, Rocal is also home to a wide variety of regional plants, flowers, and roots that are used in herbal infusions. Rocal Rose Tea, for instance, is a popular beverage made from the petals of wild roses that grow abundantly in the region's gardens. The tea has a delicate, floral taste and is often enjoyed for its calming and anti-inflammatory effects. Similarly, Rocal Hibiscus Tea, made from the vibrant red petals of hibiscus flowers, is cherished for its tart, tangy flavor and its ability to lower blood pressure and improve heart health.

Herbal teas in Rocal are often consumed throughout the day, offering both hydration and medicinal benefits. They are typically prepared using a simple method: fresh herbs are steeped in hot water for several minutes, allowing the natural oils and flavors to infuse into the water. The result is a soothing, aromatic beverage that is enjoyed either hot or cold. Many Rocal herbal teas are also sweetened with a touch of honey, which not only enhances the flavor but also adds additional health benefits, as honey is known for its antimicrobial and soothing properties.

Herbal teas are often consumed during social gatherings and family meals, where they serve as a welcoming gesture and a symbol of hospitality. It is common in Rocal culture to offer guests a cup of herbal tea upon arrival, a practice that highlights the importance of connection and sharing in the region's social fabric. The preparation of these teas is also a communal activity, with family members or neighbors gathering to brew large pots of tea and enjoy the company of one another.

The medicinal and therapeutic qualities of Rocal herbal teas are another reason for their enduring popularity. Many of the herbs used in these infusions have been recognized for their healing properties for centuries, and Rocal's herbal teas are often consumed to address a variety of health issues, from stress and insomnia to digestive problems and inflammation. These teas are considered to be a natural remedy for many ailments, offering a holistic approach to health and wellness that is deeply embedded in the region's culture.

As Rocal's herbal tea tradition continues to evolve, modern-day enthusiasts have also begun experimenting with new combinations of herbs, flowers, and fruits, creating unique blends that reflect the region's growing interest in wellness and sustainable living. These new herbal infusions often incorporate ingredients like ginger, lemon, or turmeric, which are prized for their anti-inflammatory and antioxidant properties. The fusion of traditional knowledge with modern trends ensures that herbal teas remain an integral part of Rocal's beverage culture for generations to come.

Alcoholic Delights: From Wine to Spirits

Rocal's love for beverages extends beyond non-alcoholic teas and infusions to a rich tradition of alcoholic drinks that play an essential role in the region's culinary and social life. From the ancient art of wine-making to the production of locally crafted spirits, Rocal's alcoholic delights are a celebration of the region's agricultural bounty, craftsmanship, and vibrant social culture. These drinks are not only enjoyed during festive occasions but are also an integral part of daily life, offering a taste of the region's rich history and the creativity of its people.

Rocal Wine is perhaps the most celebrated of the region's alcoholic beverages. The area's climate, which is perfect for grape cultivation, has allowed wine-making to flourish for centuries. The vineyards of Rocal are known for producing a wide variety of wines, from crisp whites to rich reds, all of which are characterized by their deep, complex flavors. The wine-making process in Rocal is a carefully guarded tradition, passed down through generations of family-owned wineries. Grapes are hand-harvested at the peak of ripeness, and the fermentation process is overseen by skilled artisans who have perfected the craft over many years. Rocal Red Wine, with its deep berry notes and smooth finish, pairs perfectly with Rocal's rich meats and savory dishes, while Rocal White Wine, with its light, citrusy flavor, is an ideal accompaniment to seafood and lighter fare.

In addition to wine, Rocal is home to a variety of traditional spirits, with Rocal Arak being one of the most popular. Arak is a clear, anise-flavored spirit that is often enjoyed as an aperitif or sipped slowly after a meal. It is made by distilling grapes or dates, with the addition of aniseed to give it its signature flavor. Arak is typically served chilled and is often diluted with water, turning the spirit a milky white. The tradition of making Arak in Rocal is centuries old, with small, family-run distilleries continuing to produce the spirit using age-old techniques. Arak is more than just a drink; it's a symbol of Rocal hospitality and is often shared among friends and family during celebratory meals.

Rocal also produces a variety of fruit-based spirits, such as Rocal Fig Liquor and Rocal Pomegranate Liqueur. These spirits are made by infusing local fruits in alcohol, creating a sweet, flavorful drink that captures the essence of Rocal's abundant harvest. The production of fruit liqueurs is a testament to the creativity and ingenuity of Rocal's artisans, who take advantage of the region's rich fruit crops to craft unique, flavorful spirits that are unlike any others found around the world.

The consumption of alcohol in Rocal is deeply intertwined with social rituals and celebrations. Whether it's a glass of wine shared with friends over a meal, a sip of Arak at a wedding, or a fruity liqueur passed around during a festival, these alcoholic beverages are a symbol of togetherness, hospitality, and the joys of life. They are consumed not only to enhance the flavor of a meal but also to create lasting memories and bonds between those who partake.

Chapter 8
The Art of Rocal Dining

Rocal's dining culture is a true reflection of the region's deep respect for food, tradition, and the people with whom it is shared. Dining in Rocal is more than simply eating—it's an art form, a time-honored practice that brings people together in a celebration of life, love, and community. Every meal, whether enjoyed with family at home or shared with friends in a bustling restaurant, is a testament to the culture's emphasis on hospitality, connection, and joy. The art of Rocal dining is built upon the pillars of generosity, intricate preparation, and respect for the ingredients that define the region's culinary heritage.

In Rocal, dining is a communal experience. Meals are rarely eaten alone; instead, they are shared with others, allowing for conversation, laughter, and a sense of togetherness. The act of serving food is just as important as the meal itself. It is customary to offer guests a place at the table, and the abundance of food often reflects the warmth and generosity of the host. The importance of sharing food is so deeply ingrained in Rocal culture that it extends beyond family gatherings to include strangers and new acquaintances, as hospitality is considered a fundamental value.

The aesthetic of Rocal dining also plays an important role. The presentation of dishes is carefully considered, with vibrant colors, fresh ingredients, and beautifully arranged plates enhancing the dining experience. A typical Rocal meal often includes multiple courses, each one designed to build upon the previous, offering a balanced and harmonious experience for the senses. From the carefully chosen spices that season each dish to the meticulous preparation that goes into every plate, Rocal dining is a reflection of the region's culinary artistry, where food becomes a canvas and a means of bringing people together in celebration.

The Role of Presentation in Rocal Cuisine

In Rocal, the presentation of food is an art form in itself, meticulously crafted to elevate the dining experience and reflect the deep cultural value placed on meals. The way a dish is presented goes beyond just making it visually appealing; it embodies the craftsmanship, care, and pride that Rocal chefs take in their culinary creations. Presentation is considered a reflection of the respect shown to the ingredients, the people who will consume the meal, and the overall dining experience. The visual appeal of a dish is as important as its taste, and every meal is carefully arranged to stimulate the senses before it even reaches the palate.

At the heart of Rocal cuisine's presentation is the use of vibrant colors. Fresh vegetables, herbs, and fruits are used to not only enhance the flavor of dishes but to create a beautiful contrast on the plate. Dishes often feature a spectrum of colors, with green from herbs like parsley and cilantro, red from tomatoes and peppers, and yellow and orange from spices such as saffron or turmeric. These colors are thoughtfully arranged to create an inviting and aesthetically pleasing presentation, symbolizing the harmony between the earth and the table.

Rocal cuisine also emphasizes intricate garnishing techniques. Dishes are often garnished with edible flowers, fresh herbs, or spices, which are carefully placed to enhance both the look and flavor of the meal. A simple bowl of stew, for example, may be topped with a dollop of yogurt and a sprig of fresh mint or a dash of paprika, adding a burst of color and a layer of complexity to the flavor profile. These garnishes are not only meant to be beautiful but are also intended to complement the dish's flavor, providing an extra dimension to the dining experience.

The traditional platings of Rocal cuisine also reflect a cultural appreciation for balance and proportion. In a typical Rocal meal, the arrangement of food on the plate is meant to create symmetry and harmony, with each element having its own space and purpose. For example, a platter of grilled lamb skewers might be arranged neatly with side dishes like fresh salad, rice, or flatbread surrounding it, allowing each component to shine individually while also coming together to form a cohesive whole. The careful division of space on the plate allows for each flavor and texture to be experienced fully, highlighting the artistry involved in both cooking and presenting the meal.

Additionally, the vessels used for serving food in Rocal culture are as important as the dish itself. Beautifully handcrafted plates, bowls, and serving trays made from clay, ceramics, or metal are often used to present meals. These vessels are chosen not only for their aesthetic value but also for their practicality in keeping food warm and enhancing the overall sensory experience of the meal. The choice of serving utensils, from elegant spoons to decorative serving forks, adds another layer of detail to the presentation, ensuring that the entire dining experience, from the first glance to the last bite, is visually pleasing and satisfying.

The importance of food presentation in Rocal cuisine is not just a modern trend—it is rooted in the region's long history of culinary artistry. Over the centuries, Rocal chefs have perfected the art of making food not just a source of nourishment but a visual delight. The careful attention to detail, the use of vibrant colors, and the thoughtful arrangement of ingredients ensure that Rocal cuisine is not only a feast for the stomach but a feast for the eyes. Every meal is a celebration of the region's rich cultural heritage and an invitation to experience the artistry that goes into every dish.

Dining Etiquette: From Family Meals to Grand Gatherings

Dining etiquette in Rocal is deeply ingrained in the culture, and it reflects the region's values of respect, hospitality, and community. The way meals are shared, the rituals surrounding food, and the manner in which people engage with each other during a meal are all important aspects of Rocal's dining traditions. From intimate family meals to grand gatherings, the dining etiquette in Rocal is designed to foster a sense of connection, honor the food, and celebrate the people gathered around the table.

Family meals in Rocal are characterized by their warmth and informality, but they are no less important in terms of etiquette. Typically, a family meal begins with a warm greeting and an invitation to sit at the table. In Rocal culture, it is common for the host to offer guests the best seats at the table and to serve them first, ensuring that everyone feels valued and respected. Meals are often shared family-style, with large platters of food placed in the center of the table for everyone to partake from. This communal approach to dining fosters a sense of unity and togetherness, allowing everyone to enjoy the food and the company in equal measure.

When it comes to etiquette at the table, Rocal's customs emphasize respect for both the food and the people around you. It is considered polite to wait for the host to begin eating before taking the first bite. It is also customary to pass dishes around the table, ensuring that everyone is able to enjoy a variety of foods. In many Rocal households, meals are eaten with the right hand, as the left hand is considered impolite for eating, although the use of utensils like forks and spoons is becoming more common in urban settings.

At grand gatherings and special occasions, dining etiquette takes on an even more formal tone. For celebrations such as weddings, religious holidays, or important family milestones, elaborate meals are prepared, and the social dynamics at the table become more structured. The seating arrangement often follows a hierarchy, with the eldest members of the family or honored guests sitting at the head of the table. It is also customary for the host to offer a special toast to mark the occasion, often with a traditional beverage like Rocal Arak or Rocal Wine. This act of toasting is symbolic of good health, happiness, and prosperity, and is an important part of the meal.

The meal is served in multiple courses, each one carefully presented and prepared with great attention to detail. Guests are expected to eat slowly, savoring each dish and enjoying the conversation. In Rocal culture, it is considered impolite to rush through a meal, as dining is not just about eating but about bonding with others and enjoying the moment. There is often an emphasis on conversation during the meal, with topics ranging from family news to local events. The table is a place for dialogue, laughter, and storytelling, and the meal itself becomes a catalyst for building and strengthening relationships.

After the meal, it is customary for the host to offer a sweet treat, often a small dessert or a fruit platter, as a final gesture of hospitality. The meal ends with a warm farewell and an invitation to return for future meals, reinforcing the strong sense of community that is so important in Rocal culture. Whether it is a casual family dinner or a lavish celebration, dining etiquette in Rocal ensures that every meal is an experience that goes beyond the food—it's about nurturing relationships, honoring traditions, and creating lasting memories.

The Importance of Hospitality in Rocal Culture

Hospitality is a cornerstone of Rocal culture, and it plays a vital role in shaping the way meals are shared, enjoyed, and celebrated. In Rocal, the act of sharing food is seen as an expression of generosity, respect, and care for others. Hospitality goes beyond simply inviting someone into your home for a meal—it is about making guests feel welcome, valued, and honored. It reflects the deep-seated belief that food is not only a means of nourishment but also a way to build connections, strengthen bonds, and foster a sense of community.

The tradition of hospitality in Rocal is deeply rooted in the region's cultural and historical practices. The offering of food to guests is considered one of the highest forms of respect. It is customary for hosts to go to great lengths to ensure that their guests are well taken care of, with food being the centerpiece of this care. Meals are often prepared with great attention to detail, and hosts will offer the best dishes, ensuring that guests are satisfied and comfortable throughout the meal.

Rocal hospitality is also about creating an atmosphere of warmth and relaxation. When guests arrive, they are often greeted with a warm welcome, offered a refreshing drink, and invited to sit and relax before the meal. The dining table is set with care, often adorned with beautiful dishes and tableware, creating an inviting and pleasant environment. It is common for meals to be served in generous portions, reflecting the host's desire to share abundance and ensure that no one leaves the table hungry. The act of offering food is symbolic of the host's desire to nurture and care for their guests, and it is a gesture that is deeply appreciated in Rocal culture.

The significance of hospitality extends beyond the individual meal—it is a reflection of the broader social values that define Rocal society. In Rocal culture, hospitality is seen as a way of fostering relationships and strengthening social bonds. Sharing food with others is a way of showing that you care, and it is often used as a means of forging new connections or reaffirming old ones. This is why meals in Rocal are often shared in large groups, where families, friends, and even strangers gather to enjoy food together, exchange stories, and build relationships. It is common for Rocal hospitality to extend beyond the meal itself, with guests invited to return in the future for more gatherings, further reinforcing the sense of community and connection.

The emphasis on hospitality is also seen in the preparation of special foods for guests. Rocal hosts often prepare elaborate feasts or special dishes that are reserved for important occasions or when welcoming guests. These dishes are prepared with great care, using the finest ingredients and cooking techniques to ensure that every guest feels honored. Whether it's a large family gathering, a celebration, or a simple get-together, Rocal meals are always about sharing, enjoying, and creating lasting memories.

Ultimately, hospitality in Rocal culture is not just about offering food—it is about creating an experience of warmth, connection, and respect. The act of sharing food becomes a way of fostering community, building relationships, and showing kindness to others. It is a vital part of the cultural fabric, and it is through hospitality that Rocal's deep-rooted values of generosity, respect, and love are passed down through generations, ensuring that every meal shared is a meaningful and cherished occasion.

Chapter 9
Cooking Techniques: From the Kitchen to the Table

The art of cooking in Rocal is an intricate and deeply rooted tradition that combines time-honored techniques with an evolving culinary creativity. From humble family kitchens to grand banquet halls, the techniques used in Rocal cuisine reflect a profound respect for ingredients, flavor balance, and the culture of sharing. The process of cooking in Rocal is not simply about preparing food; it is a ritual, a form of expression, and an opportunity to connect with the land, the seasons, and the generations that have passed down their culinary knowledge. Every dish is a reflection of this history, shaped by both ancient practices and modern innovations.

In Rocal kitchens, cooking is an intentional, methodical process that begins long before the first ingredients are chopped. The emphasis is placed on sourcing the best, freshest produce, meats, and spices, ensuring that each dish is as flavorful and vibrant as possible. From the moment a meal is conceived, Rocal cooks are guided by a deep understanding of their ingredients—the way they should be handled, prepared, and combined to bring out their fullest potential. Whether it's the precise art of braising lamb to perfection or the delicate folding of pastry dough, Rocal cooking is rooted in both tradition and technique.

The methods used in Rocal kitchens range from slow-braised stews that allow the flavors to meld over hours to the quick and precise techniques required to prepare the perfect grilled fish. The region's diverse range of techniques highlights a versatility that reflects the many facets of Rocal life—from the rustic simplicity of home-cooked meals to the elaborate dishes served during grand celebrations. Slow cooking, searing, grilling, baking, and even fermentation are techniques often employed, each contributing to the dish's complexity and depth. Grilling, in particular, is a revered practice, especially when it comes to preparing meats and vegetables, giving them a smoky, charred flavor that is unmistakable in Rocal cuisine.

Yet, while the techniques are often steeped in tradition, Rocal chefs embrace modern innovations to refine and enhance their cooking. The introduction of contemporary appliances and technology allows for greater control over heat, texture, and timing, making it possible to perfect dishes that would have once taken hours of hands-on attention. The fusion of ancient techniques with contemporary methods helps create dishes that are both timeless and forward-thinking.

From the kitchen to the table, Rocal cooking is an immersive experience. Each step in the preparation, from the choice of utensils to the arrangement of dishes, plays a role in how the food is experienced. The presentation is just as important as the preparation, ensuring that the visual appeal of a dish matches the depth of its flavor. This chapter explores the techniques that define Rocal cuisine, highlighting how they come together to create meals that are not just food, but an expression of culture, history, and community. Whether it's a simple meal shared between family members or a grand feast prepared for a special occasion, the process of cooking in Rocal is a journey from the heart of the kitchen to the table, creating a deep, lasting connection with every bite.

Ancient Methods Still in Use

The culinary traditions of Rocal are built upon centuries of history, with ancient cooking methods still in use today. These traditional techniques have been passed down from generation to generation, shaped by both the region's natural environment and the experiences of its people. While modern appliances and methods have found their way into Rocal kitchens, the core of Rocal cuisine remains deeply rooted in ancient practices that emphasize simplicity, patience, and respect for the ingredients. These methods allow the flavors of the region's produce, meats, and spices to shine through in their purest forms.

One of the most revered ancient methods still in use is slow-cooking. Slow-cooked stews, braises, and soups have been staples of Rocal cuisine for centuries. These dishes are often cooked for several hours, allowing the flavors to meld together and the ingredients to break down, creating rich, comforting meals. For example, Rocal Lamb Stew, a beloved dish in the region, involves simmering lamb in a broth with vegetables and aromatic spices over a low flame for hours. The slow cooking process not only tenderizes the meat but also extracts all the flavors, infusing the dish with depth and complexity.

The art of grilling is another ancient technique that remains essential in Rocal kitchens. Grilling meats, fish, and vegetables over open flames is a practice that dates back to the region's earliest inhabitants. The smoky flavors imparted by the grill are a hallmark of Rocal cuisine, and the method is often used to prepare lamb skewers, fish, and even fruits like peaches and melons. The traditional use of charcoal in grilling adds a distinct flavor profile, which cannot be replicated by modern electric grills. This cooking method requires skill and experience, with the heat and timing needing to be carefully controlled to ensure the perfect level of char without overcooking the food.

In addition to grilling and slow cooking, Rocal's use of clay pots and open hearths is a testament to its ancient culinary traditions. Clay pots have been used for thousands of years to cook stews, soups, and rice dishes. These vessels distribute heat evenly, allowing the food to cook slowly and retain its moisture and flavors. Cooking over an open hearth, whether for roasting meats or baking bread, also remains a common practice in rural areas, providing an authentic and rustic cooking experience.

Preserving food through drying and fermenting is another technique rooted in ancient Rocal culture. Drying fruits, vegetables, and herbs was once necessary to ensure that food could be stored for the colder months, and many families still follow this tradition today. Likewise, fermentation methods are used to create a variety of pickles, preserved vegetables, and dairy products such as yogurt. These fermented foods not only enhance the flavors of dishes but also contribute to the region's rich food culture, connecting present-day cooks with their ancestors.

The continued use of these ancient cooking methods in Rocal kitchens is a testament to the resilience and adaptability of the region's culinary heritage. These techniques not only preserve the authentic flavors of the past but also allow for the creation of dishes that continue to nourish the soul, as they have done for generations. In Rocal, cooking is more than just a means of sustenance; it is an expression of cultural identity, passed down through the ages and still cherished today.

Modern Appliances Meet Traditional Recipes

While Rocal's ancient culinary techniques remain essential to its food culture, the region's kitchens have not been immune to the influence of modern technology. The advent of modern appliances has revolutionized the way food is prepared, allowing Rocal chefs to combine traditional recipes with contemporary tools, enhancing both efficiency and precision in the kitchen. Rather than abandoning their time-honored methods, Rocal chefs have found ways to integrate modern appliances into their cooking, creating a fusion of the old and the new that enhances the overall culinary experience.

One of the most significant advancements in Rocal kitchens is the introduction of electric ovens, gas stoves, and pressure cookers. These appliances have made cooking faster and more efficient, without sacrificing the integrity of traditional recipes. For example, slow-cooked stews, such as Rocal Beef and Vegetable Stew, which would traditionally require hours of simmering over an open flame or in a clay pot, can now be prepared in a fraction of the time using a pressure cooker. The pressure cooker retains the depth of flavor achieved through slow cooking, while also tenderizing the meat and vegetables quickly, making it an invaluable tool in modern Rocal kitchens.

Similarly, the use of induction cooktops and gas stoves has allowed chefs to more precisely control the heat, ensuring that delicate dishes like Rocal Grilled Fish or Rocal Rice Pilaf are cooked to perfection. The ability to control temperature more effectively allows chefs to achieve the ideal texture and flavor, something that was far more challenging when cooking over open flames. While the art of grilling over charcoal remains deeply embedded in Rocal tradition, many chefs now use modern grills with adjustable temperature settings, making the process more precise while still retaining the smoky, charred flavors that are central to the region's culinary identity.

The introduction of food processors and blenders has also had a profound impact on Rocal cooking. These tools allow for quicker preparation of ingredients, whether it's finely chopping herbs for a fresh Rocal Herb Salad or blending spices into a smooth paste for a curry or stew. The convenience of modern appliances has enabled Rocal chefs to experiment with new textures and flavors, while still adhering to the traditional ingredients and recipes that define the cuisine. The ability to quickly grind spices, chop vegetables, and mix dough has made meal preparation more efficient, especially in busy kitchens or when preparing large quantities for gatherings.

Modern refrigeration has also transformed the way Rocal cooks store and preserve ingredients. Fresh produce, dairy, and meats can now be kept at their peak freshness, allowing for year-round access to ingredients that were once seasonal. The ability to store herbs, meats, and fish for longer periods has expanded the variety of dishes that can be prepared, even outside of traditional growing seasons. This has not only enhanced the culinary versatility of Rocal but also allowed chefs to maintain a higher level of consistency and quality in their dishes.

While modern appliances have certainly made cooking in Rocal more efficient, they have not replaced the deep cultural value placed on traditional methods. Instead, they complement and enhance these methods, allowing chefs to preserve the authenticity of Rocal cuisine while embracing innovation. The result is a unique blend of old and new, where the integrity of traditional recipes is maintained, and modern conveniences allow for greater creativity and precision in the kitchen.

Rocal's Approach to Preserving Flavor

In Rocal cuisine, preserving the natural flavors of ingredients is paramount. From ancient cooking methods to modern innovations, the region's culinary approach emphasizes techniques that allow the true essence of each ingredient to shine. The preservation of flavor is not just about the way food is prepared, but also about the care and attention paid to the sourcing, handling, and storage of ingredients. In Rocal, flavor preservation is an art that combines respect for nature's bounty with a deep understanding of cooking techniques, ensuring that each dish is a celebration of the region's rich agricultural heritage.

One of the key ways that Rocal preserves flavor is through the use of slow cooking and low-temperature methods. Whether it's slow-braising lamb in a fragrant broth or simmering a pot of vegetables for hours, these methods allow the ingredients to release their natural juices and flavors over time. Slow cooking helps to break down tougher cuts of meat, making them tender and infusing them with rich, complex flavors. This process is especially important in Rocal stews, soups, and rice dishes, where the depth of flavor achieved through slow cooking is what defines the dish. The slow and steady cooking process also helps to retain the nutrients and natural characteristics of the ingredients, ensuring that the dish is both flavorful and nourishing.

Another important method for preserving flavor in Rocal is the use of herbs and spices. Fresh herbs such as mint, parsley, and cilantro are used generously in Rocal cuisine to enhance the natural flavors of the food. These herbs are often added at the end of the cooking process, preserving their freshness and aromatic qualities. Spices like cumin, coriander, cinnamon, and saffron are also integral to Rocal's flavor profile. The careful toasting and grinding of whole spices is a technique that allows their essential oils to be released, infusing the dish with a deep, aromatic flavor that cannot be achieved with pre-ground spices.

Fermentation is another key aspect of flavor preservation in Rocal cuisine. Fermented foods, such as pickled vegetables, yogurt, and sourdough bread, play an important role in balancing the richness of other dishes. The tangy acidity of fermented foods acts as a counterpoint to the heaviness of meat-based stews and dishes, adding brightness and complexity. In Rocal, fermentation is not only a way of preserving food but also a way of enhancing flavor. The process of fermenting vegetables, fruits, and dairy products develops unique flavors that are impossible to replicate through other methods.

Rocal also preserves the flavors of seasonal ingredients by drying and smoking. Fruits such as figs, apricots, and tomatoes are dried to preserve them for use during the off-season. The drying process intensifies the natural sweetness of the fruit, making them ideal for use in stews, desserts, and salads. Smoking, especially when it comes to meats and fish, is another traditional technique that imparts a distinct flavor to the food. Smoked meats and fish are integral to Rocal's culinary culture, offering a rich, smoky depth that enhances the overall taste of the dish.

Finally, Rocal chefs also take great care in sourcing ingredients locally, ensuring that the food is as fresh and flavorful as possible. By using seasonal produce and supporting local farmers and markets, Rocal cuisine remains deeply connected to the land. The freshness of the ingredients is key to preserving their natural flavors, and the region's emphasis on local sourcing allows for a wide variety of high-quality ingredients to be used throughout the year.

In Rocal, the preservation of flavor is a meticulous process that values the integrity of ingredients and cooking techniques. From slow-cooking and fermenting to using fresh herbs and spices, Rocal's approach to preserving flavor allows the true essence of each ingredient to shine through in every dish. Whether it's the deep, complex flavors of a slow-braised stew or the vibrant freshness of a herb-filled salad, Rocal cuisine ensures that every meal is an unforgettable experience, highlighting the beauty and authenticity of the ingredients at its core.

Chapter 10
Rocal Cuisine in the Modern World

Rocal cuisine, rooted in centuries-old traditions, has long been revered for its deep flavors, complex techniques, and rich cultural heritage. As the world continues to evolve, Rocal cuisine faces both new challenges and exciting opportunities in the modern culinary landscape. The way Rocal food is experienced, prepared, and shared today is shaped by a blend of tradition and innovation, as the region's rich culinary history meets the fast-paced, interconnected world of contemporary dining. This chapter explores how Rocal cuisine has navigated the changing tides of globalization, technology, and evolving consumer preferences, and how it continues to thrive in the modern world.

One of the most significant developments in the modern world of Rocal cuisine is the increasing availability and popularity of its dishes outside of the region. Globalization has allowed the flavors, ingredients, and techniques of Rocal cooking to reach far beyond its borders, bringing the region's culinary treasures to new audiences. Rocal food is now being celebrated in major cities worldwide, with international chefs incorporating Rocal spices, herbs, and cooking methods into their own menus. The rise of food tourism has also contributed to this global exposure, with people traveling to Rocal to experience the authenticity and richness of its cuisine firsthand. The fusion of Rocal flavors with other global cuisines is giving rise to new interpretations of traditional dishes, creating a modern and dynamic culinary scene that blends the old with the new.

At the same time, Rocal cuisine has embraced modern technology and innovations, reshaping the way meals are prepared and enjoyed. Advances in kitchen appliances, cooking techniques, and food preservation have enabled chefs to elevate traditional dishes while maintaining the integrity of the flavors. For example, the use of precision cooking techniques, like sous-vide, has allowed Rocal chefs to achieve a level of consistency and control that was once impossible with traditional methods. However, while these innovations are valuable, many chefs in Rocal continue to rely on time-honored practices, ensuring that the essence of the cuisine is preserved.

Moreover, in the modern world, there is an increasing focus on sustainability and ethical food sourcing, and Rocal cuisine has adapted to these changing values. Local and seasonal ingredients, often organically grown, are prioritized in Rocal kitchens, reflecting a deep respect for the environment and the region's agricultural heritage. This shift aligns with global movements toward sustainable eating, which seeks to minimize food waste, reduce environmental footprints, and support local farmers.

In this chapter, we will explore how Rocal cuisine is adapting to and thriving in the modern world. Whether it is through the global popularity of its dishes, the incorporation of new technologies in food preparation, or the embrace of sustainability, Rocal food continues to be a dynamic force in the global culinary scene. The evolution of Rocal cuisine represents a perfect balance of honoring its past while embracing the possibilities of the future, ensuring that its culinary traditions remain relevant for generations to come.

Fusion and Innovation in the Rocal Kitchen

The evolution of Rocal cuisine in the modern world is deeply rooted in its ability to blend tradition with innovation. While the region's culinary practices remain firmly grounded in ancient methods passed down through generations, the infusion of modern culinary techniques and global influences has led to the development of exciting new variations of traditional dishes. Fusion and innovation have become driving forces in the Rocal kitchen, helping the cuisine evolve in response to global trends, changing tastes, and new culinary technologies, while still maintaining its cultural essence.

Fusion in the Rocal kitchen is not just about blending ingredients from different cultures, but about combining the unique flavors and techniques of Rocal with the culinary principles of other regions. The heart of Rocal cuisine lies in its vibrant spices, fresh herbs, and rich textures, all of which lend themselves beautifully to innovative twists. By incorporating ingredients from global food cultures—such as spices from India, fresh produce from the Mediterranean, and even modern techniques from European and Asian kitchens—Rocal chefs have found ways to expand the boundaries of their culinary traditions while still honoring the essence of their roots.

One of the most visible examples of fusion in the Rocal kitchen is the use of traditional ingredients in new ways. For instance, the beloved Rocal Lamb Stew, typically slow-cooked with herbs and spices over a long period, may be adapted with modern elements such as sous-vide cooking, which allows the meat to retain its tenderness and deep flavor while reducing cooking time. Similarly, classic dishes such as Rocal Grilled Fish, which relies on slow grilling over charcoal, can be innovated by introducing global marinades, such as soy-based sauces from East Asia or citrus-based dressings inspired by Latin American cuisine, infusing the dish with both the essence of Rocal's grilling tradition and new layers of flavor.

Rocal chefs are also increasingly experimenting with the use of non-traditional ingredients in familiar dishes. The use of plant-based proteins, for example, is gaining popularity, driven by global movements toward sustainable eating and the growing demand for plant-based options. In the Rocal kitchen, dishes traditionally centered around lamb or beef, such as Rocal Lamb Skewers or Beef Stew, are being reimagined using plant-based substitutes like lentils, chickpeas, or even lab-grown meat alternatives. These modern innovations allow chefs to stay connected with global dietary trends while preserving the cultural significance of Rocal's iconic flavors.

Moreover, Rocal cuisine has embraced the growing interest in local and organic farming practices. The trend toward sustainability has encouraged many chefs in Rocal to experiment with farm-to-table techniques, sourcing ingredients that are organically grown or harvested through sustainable methods. This approach not only ensures that the dishes are fresh and flavorful but also promotes an ethical relationship with the land. In Rocal kitchens, this focus on sustainability can be seen in the growing popularity of dishes that incorporate locally sourced vegetables, wild herbs, and meats from ethically raised animals, all while minimizing food waste and reducing the ecological footprint of the kitchen.

Incorporating modern culinary techniques has also been a game-changer for Rocal cuisine. The use of precision cooking methods, such as sous-vide, fermentation, and molecular gastronomy, has allowed chefs to experiment with textures, flavors, and presentation in ways that were previously unimaginable. For instance, sous-vide cooking, which involves cooking food in a vacuum-sealed bag at a low, controlled temperature, allows for dishes such as Rocal Lamb, traditionally slow-cooked, to reach new levels of tenderness and flavor without the need for hours of preparation. Similarly, molecular gastronomy techniques, such as using liquid nitrogen to freeze ingredients or creating foams and gels, have been introduced to Rocal desserts and beverages, adding a layer of modern sophistication to traditional sweets like Rocal Baklava and Rice Pudding.

The blending of modern technology with traditional methods is not just about creating novelty dishes but is rooted in the desire to elevate the flavors, textures, and overall dining experience. Chefs are finding new ways to extract flavors and intensify the essence of ingredients using modern tools, while still honoring the traditional techniques that have long defined Rocal cuisine.

The Global Influence of Rocal Dishes

Rocal cuisine has made significant strides in gaining global recognition, as its flavors and culinary techniques capture the attention of food enthusiasts and chefs worldwide. The rich and complex flavors, aromatic spices, and inventive combinations found in Rocal dishes have resonated deeply with diverse palates, making the cuisine not just a regional delight but a globally appreciated culinary tradition. The influence of Rocal cuisine can be seen in restaurants around the world, where chefs incorporate Rocal ingredients and techniques into their menus, creating exciting fusions that showcase the adaptability and appeal of Rocal dishes.

One of the key factors driving the global influence of Rocal cuisine is the increasing popularity of spices and herbs, which have been central to Rocal cooking for centuries. Spices like cumin, coriander, saffron, and cinnamon, which form the backbone of Rocal cuisine, have found their way into the kitchens of chefs around the world. These spices have transcended regional boundaries and are now used in global cuisine, from Mediterranean and Middle Eastern dishes to Western and Asian fusion cooking. The warmth and depth that these spices impart to Rocal dishes have contributed to the growing admiration for the cuisine's complex flavor profiles.

Furthermore, the global interest in healthy eating and plant-based diets has led to the exploration of Rocal cuisine's emphasis on fresh vegetables, legumes, and grains. Dishes such as Rocal Lentil Stew or Chickpea Salad, made from locally sourced produce and legumes, have gained traction in restaurants worldwide. The simplicity and wholesomeness of these dishes, which focus on plant-based ingredients, align with the global trend toward sustainable eating and vegetarian diets, making Rocal cuisine an attractive option for health-conscious consumers.

The diversity of Rocal's food culture also makes it highly adaptable to a variety of international culinary styles. For instance, Rocal Grilled Lamb, traditionally prepared over an open fire or charcoal, has influenced the grilling techniques used in Mediterranean and Latin American cooking. Similarly, Rocal's savory stews and rice dishes have been adapted by chefs in other parts of the world, combining them with local ingredients and spices to create fusion dishes that reflect both the influence of Rocal and the global culinary trends.

The rise of food tourism has also contributed to the growing popularity of Rocal cuisine. Tourists visiting Rocal's bustling markets and renowned eateries are eager to experience the flavors of the region firsthand, further driving the global interest in its dishes. As food tourism continues to grow, Rocal cuisine has gained a reputation as a must-try culinary experience, attracting food lovers from around the world who are eager to savor its authentic flavors.

Social media and food blogging have also played a significant role in the global spread of Rocal dishes. Platforms like Instagram, YouTube, and food blogs have allowed chefs and home cooks to showcase Rocal cuisine to a wider audience. Photos and videos of dishes like Rocal Baklava, Lamb Stew, and Grilled Fish have gone viral, inspiring home cooks and chefs worldwide to try their hand at recreating Rocal dishes in their own kitchens. These platforms have democratized food culture, allowing Rocal cuisine to reach a much broader audience than ever before.

In the world of fine dining, Rocal cuisine has also gained a place in Michelin-starred restaurants, with chefs experimenting with Rocal ingredients and techniques to create innovative and globally influenced dishes. These restaurants have played a key role in elevating Rocal cuisine to international recognition, blending Rocal culinary traditions with modern techniques and presentation to appeal to global tastes. As Rocal cuisine continues to be celebrated in high-end restaurants around the world, its influence on the global culinary stage will only continue to grow.

The Future of Rocal Gastronomy

The future of Rocal gastronomy is one of exciting possibilities, as the region's rich culinary heritage continues to evolve in response to global trends, technological innovations, and an ever-changing food landscape. Rocal cuisine, with its deep connection to tradition and respect for local ingredients, is well-positioned to thrive in the modern world while maintaining its authenticity. As new generations of chefs and home cooks take on the mantle of preserving and innovating Rocal food, the cuisine will continue to evolve, embracing both the opportunities of the future and the timelessness of its culinary roots.

One of the most significant trends shaping the future of Rocal gastronomy is the growing focus on sustainability. As the global food industry increasingly turns to sustainable practices, Rocal chefs are incorporating these principles into their kitchens. The emphasis on using local, organic ingredients, minimizing food waste, and supporting ethical farming practices aligns perfectly with Rocal cuisine's long-standing traditions of respecting the land and its resources. In the future, we can expect Rocal cuisine to continue to lead the way in sustainable food practices, with more chefs choosing to focus on seasonality, organic produce, and environmentally friendly cooking methods.

Innovation will also play a major role in the future of Rocal gastronomy. As new cooking technologies emerge, Rocal chefs will find new ways to adapt these innovations while preserving the core techniques that define the cuisine. The integration of digital tools, precision cooking techniques, and even artificial intelligence in the kitchen may transform how Rocal dishes are prepared, presented, and experienced. However, the key challenge will be to maintain the balance between embracing technology and staying true to the traditional methods that give Rocal cuisine its unique flavor and character.

Additionally, the future of Rocal gastronomy will likely see an even greater fusion of global influences. The region's increasing popularity on the global culinary stage means that Rocal cuisine will continue to interact with other food cultures, creating exciting new combinations of flavors and techniques. While fusion has already been a hallmark of Rocal cuisine, the future will bring even more opportunities for cross-cultural collaboration, resulting in dishes that represent a harmonious blend of the old and the new.

Finally, the future of Rocal gastronomy will continue to be shaped by the growing interest in food tourism and the rise of experiential dining. As travelers seek authentic, immersive culinary experiences, Rocal cuisine will remain a sought-after destination for food lovers from around the world. Restaurants, food markets, and cooking schools in Rocal will continue to draw visitors eager to explore the flavors and traditions of the region, ensuring that Rocal gastronomy maintains its place on the global food map.

In conclusion, the future of Rocal cuisine is bright and full of promise. By embracing both innovation and tradition, sustainability and creativity, Rocal gastronomy will continue to evolve while honoring the cultural richness and flavors that have defined it for centuries. As the world becomes increasingly interconnected, Rocal's culinary traditions will remain a vital part of the global food scene, offering a taste of the region's unique history, culture, and flavors to the world.

Chapter 11
Regional Variations: Exploring Rocal's Diversity

Rocal's culinary landscape is a reflection of its diverse geography, history, and cultural influences. Spanning from lush, fertile valleys to rugged mountains and sun-kissed coastal regions, Rocal is home to a wide variety of landscapes, each of which contributes its own unique ingredients, techniques, and traditions to the broader culinary fabric of the region. From the rich, earthy flavors of the highlands to the fresh, light dishes of the coastal areas, the regional variations in Rocal cuisine offer an exciting exploration of diversity, with each area having its own distinct identity.

The heart of Rocal's diversity lies in its people and the various cultures that have shaped the region over millennia. Historically, Rocal has been a crossroads for various civilizations, each of which has left its mark on the local food culture. The agricultural practices of these different groups, combined with the influences of trade routes and migration, have resulted in a rich fusion of flavors, ingredients, and cooking techniques. As a result, Rocal's food culture is not monolithic; rather, it is a vibrant mosaic of regional variations, each with its own history and evolution.

The mountainous regions of Rocal, for example, are known for their hearty and robust dishes. In these high-altitude areas, where the climate is cooler and harsher, the food tends to be richer and more substantial. Meat, particularly lamb and beef, is a central component of these dishes, often slow-cooked in stews or grilled over open flames. Root vegetables like potatoes, carrots, and turnips are common, as they thrive in the cooler temperatures and are ideal for slow cooking. Spices like rosemary, thyme, and garlic are used generously to flavor the dishes, providing a deep, aromatic base that complements the richness of the meats. This mountainous region is also known for its dairy products, including cheeses and butters, which are often used in cooking or served alongside meals.

In contrast, the coastal regions of Rocal boast a cuisine that is lighter and fresher, influenced by the abundance of seafood found in the surrounding waters. Fish, shellfish, and sea vegetables take center stage in these coastal dishes, often prepared with simple, clean flavors that highlight the natural sweetness of the ocean. Grilled fish, seafood stews, and raw preparations such as ceviche are staples in these regions, with ingredients like citrus, olive oil, and herbs like basil and mint used to complement the seafood. The coastal regions also have a rich tradition of fruit-based desserts, with fresh tropical fruits like pomegranates, figs, and citrus fruits playing a central role in creating sweet, refreshing treats.

The fertile plains and valleys of Rocal offer a different culinary experience altogether. Known for its abundance of fresh produce, the food in these areas is characterized by an emphasis on vegetables, grains, and legumes. Dishes made with lentils, chickpeas, and beans are common, often accompanied by rice or flatbreads. The use of locally grown herbs and spices such as cumin, coriander, and paprika adds flavor and depth to these dishes, while olive oil and yogurt are frequently used to create rich, flavorful sauces. The agricultural richness of the plains allows for a variety of seasonal vegetables to be incorporated into meals, making the cuisine in these regions light, vibrant, and ever-changing with the seasons.

Rocal's diverse landscapes and climate zones are not the only factors that influence regional cuisine; cultural and social practices play an equally important role. The way food is prepared, served, and enjoyed varies from region to region, with different customs surrounding meals. In some regions, food is prepared in large communal pots and served family-style, emphasizing shared experiences and the importance of togetherness. In other areas, more formal, plated meals are common, reflecting the region's history and influence from external culinary traditions.

In this chapter, we will dive deeper into the regional variations that make Rocal cuisine so dynamic. By exploring the distinct flavors, techniques, and traditions of each area, we will uncover the complexity of Rocal's food culture and how it reflects the region's rich history and diverse influences. Whether it's the hearty stews of the mountains, the fresh seafood of the coast, or the vibrant vegetable-based dishes of the plains, Rocal's diversity offers something for every palate, making it one of the most exciting culinary destinations in the world.

North vs South: Culinary Differences in Rocal

Rocal's culinary identity is shaped by its regional differences, particularly those between the northern and southern regions of the country. These two regions, though sharing a common cultural foundation, have evolved distinct culinary traditions, influenced by geography, climate, history, and local ingredients. The culinary divide between the North and South of Rocal is a reflection of how different landscapes and climates can foster unique culinary practices, ingredients, and flavors, creating two distinct yet complementary cuisines within the same nation.

The Northern regions of Rocal, characterized by their mountainous terrain and cooler climates, tend to emphasize hearty, robust dishes that can withstand the challenges of the colder environment. In the North, the emphasis is on rich, savory meats such as lamb, beef, and goat, often prepared through slow-cooking techniques like braising and stewing. The cold temperatures of the highlands make these meats ideal for long cooking times, allowing for the development of deep, complex flavors. Stews, such as Rocal Lamb Stew and Beef Braise with Root Vegetables, are staples in the North, where they are often cooked for hours, allowing the meat to become tender and the flavors to meld. These stews are traditionally served with a side of flatbread or rice, and sometimes accompanied by yogurt or a drizzle of olive oil.

The Northern regions of Rocal also have a tradition of dairy farming, which contributes to the prevalence of dairy products in local cuisine. Cheese, butter, and yogurt are commonly used in the North, adding richness to the food. Northern specialties like Rocal Cheese-filled Pastries and Creamy Lamb and Potato Casserole feature generous amounts of dairy, enhancing the natural flavors of the meats and vegetables. Additionally, the cooler climate of the North is ideal for the production of root vegetables like potatoes, carrots, and turnips, which are frequently used in hearty dishes and stews. These vegetables thrive in the colder temperatures and are perfect for slow-cooked meals that provide warmth and sustenance during the long winters.

In contrast, the Southern regions of Rocal are blessed with a warmer climate, fertile soils, and proximity to the coast, which shapes the cuisine in a very different way. The South's cuisine is lighter, fresher, and more reliant on seafood and vegetables. Fish, shellfish, and other marine delicacies are integral to Southern cooking, with dishes like Grilled Fish with Citrus and Seafood Stew dominating the local food scene. The use of fresh seafood reflects the South's access to the bountiful waters surrounding Rocal, making it a key feature of the cuisine. The Southern regions also boast a variety of fruits and vegetables that thrive in the warmer climate, such as tomatoes, olives, eggplant, and citrus fruits, all of which feature prominently in Southern dishes. Fresh salads, like Rocal Mediterranean Salad, made with cucumbers, tomatoes, olives, and feta cheese, are common in the South, offering a light and refreshing accompaniment to the heavier meat-based dishes of the North.

The contrast between North and South is not only evident in the types of ingredients used but also in the cooking methods employed. In the South, grilling and roasting are common techniques, especially for seafood and vegetables. Dishes like Grilled Shrimp with Lemon and Herbs or Roasted Eggplant with Garlic and Olive Oil showcase the region's preference for simple, clean cooking methods that allow the natural flavors of the ingredients to shine. The use of olive oil, herbs like basil and oregano, and citrus is prevalent in Southern cooking, adding brightness and a Mediterranean flair to the dishes.

One of the most important distinctions between Northern and Southern Rocal cuisine is the way food is enjoyed and served. In the North, meals are often larger, more formal affairs, particularly during celebrations or special occasions. The dishes are hearty, filling, and designed to keep people warm during the colder months. In the South, meals are often lighter and more communal, with a focus on fresh, seasonal ingredients. Meals are typically served family-style, with dishes being shared by everyone at the table, reflecting the social nature of dining in the Southern regions.

While there are distinct culinary differences between the North and South of Rocal, it is important to note that both regions share a deep connection to the land, its agricultural heritage, and the principles of hospitality. Whether it's the rich, comforting stews of the North or the fresh, vibrant seafood dishes of the South, both regions reflect Rocal's commitment to using high-quality, locally sourced ingredients and creating meals that bring people together. The North and South may have different approaches to food, but both celebrate the region's rich culinary diversity and showcase the beauty of Rocal's varied landscapes and cultures.

The Impact of Geography on Rocal Cuisine

The geography of Rocal plays a crucial role in shaping its cuisine, as the country's diverse landscapes, climates, and natural resources have contributed to the development of a rich culinary tradition. From the rugged mountains in the north to the fertile plains and the coastal regions in the south, the geographic features of Rocal provide a unique backdrop for the food culture, influencing everything from the ingredients available to the cooking methods used.

Rocal's varied topography has a direct impact on the types of crops and livestock that thrive in different regions. The northern mountainous areas, with their cooler temperatures and rocky terrain, are better suited to grazing animals like sheep, goats, and cattle. These animals provide meat, dairy, and wool, all of which are central to the cuisine of the northern regions. The cold climate also allows for the cultivation of root vegetables such as potatoes, carrots, and beets, which are commonly used in hearty stews and casseroles. The use of slow-cooking methods, such as braising and stewing, is particularly suited to the northern geography, as these techniques allow tougher cuts of meat to become tender and absorb the deep flavors of herbs, spices, and vegetables.

In contrast, the southern regions of Rocal benefit from a warmer climate, fertile soil, and access to the Mediterranean Sea. This geography allows for the cultivation of a wide variety of fruits and vegetables, such as tomatoes, citrus fruits, olives, and eggplants. The warm temperatures and abundant sunlight create an ideal environment for growing crops that thrive in hot climates, and as a result, Southern Rocal cuisine is characterized by its light, fresh flavors, often incorporating seafood, olive oil, and fresh herbs like basil, thyme, and oregano. The proximity to the sea also influences the types of fish and shellfish used in Southern cooking. Seafood is an essential component of the region's diet, with dishes like grilled fish, seafood stews, and fish-based appetizers taking center stage in the South's culinary repertoire.

The geography of Rocal has also influenced the way food is prepared and cooked. In the northern regions, where temperatures can drop significantly, traditional cooking methods such as slow cooking, roasting, and baking have evolved to suit the colder environment. In these areas, the preservation of food through methods such as curing, smoking, and pickling is common, as these techniques help to extend the shelf life of ingredients during the harsh winters. In contrast, the southern regions, with their warmer temperatures and abundance of fresh produce, favor grilling, roasting, and sautéing, techniques that highlight the fresh, vibrant flavors of the local ingredients.

Rocal's diverse geography also shapes the culinary experiences of its people. In the northern regions, meals are often more substantial and are designed to provide warmth and nourishment in the colder months. The emphasis is on hearty, filling dishes that can be enjoyed in larger quantities, such as stews, roasts, and casseroles. These meals are typically enjoyed in a family or community setting, with a focus on sharing and bonding over a rich, satisfying meal. In the southern regions, where the climate is warmer and the ingredients lighter, meals are often enjoyed in a more informal, communal style. Dining in the South is a social event, with fresh seafood, salads, and light appetizers being shared among friends and family, often accompanied by wine or spirits.

Geography also plays a key role in determining the availability of certain ingredients throughout the year. In the north, the cooler climate means that certain crops and herbs are available only during specific seasons, with winter being a time for preserved meats, root vegetables, and hearty grains. The Southern regions, on the other hand, have a longer growing season, allowing for a wider variety of fresh fruits, vegetables, and herbs to be available year-round. This seasonal variation in ingredients has led to a strong tradition of using what is locally available and in season, with many dishes evolving to reflect the rhythms of the land.

The impact of geography on Rocal cuisine is undeniable. From the types of crops and livestock that thrive in different regions to the cooking techniques and seasonal variations in ingredients, the geography of Rocal shapes every aspect of its culinary tradition. Whether it's the rich, warming dishes of the northern highlands or the fresh, vibrant flavors of the southern coast, Rocal's food culture is inextricably linked to the land, its climate, and its natural resources. The diversity of Rocal's geography ensures that the cuisine remains dynamic, evolving with the changing seasons and landscapes, while still honoring the deep cultural traditions that define the region.

How Local Ingredients Shape Regional Dishes

In Rocal, the ingredients used in each region are not just key to the flavor of the dishes but are a direct reflection of the local geography, climate, and agricultural practices. Local ingredients play an integral role in shaping regional dishes, providing the foundation for a cuisine that is deeply connected to the land and its resources. From the fertile plains of the South to the mountainous terrain in the North, the ingredients available in each region have given rise to unique dishes that celebrate the natural bounty of the area.

The northern regions of Rocal, with their cooler climates and rugged terrain, are home to ingredients that are hardy and able to withstand harsh conditions. Meat, particularly lamb, beef, and goat, is a central feature of northern Rocal cuisine. The livestock that thrives in the highlands are well-suited to the colder temperatures, and their meat is used in a variety of dishes, from stews to grilled cuts. These meats are often paired with root vegetables like potatoes, carrots, and parsnips, which grow well in the cooler climate. The northern regions also produce dairy products, including cheese, butter, and yogurt, which add richness and flavor to the dishes. The combination of hearty meats, root vegetables, and dairy creates the base for many traditional northern Rocal dishes, which are often slow-cooked to allow the flavors to develop over time.

In the Southern regions, the climate is warmer, and the fertile soil allows for the cultivation of a wide variety of fruits, vegetables, and herbs. Ingredients like tomatoes, eggplants, olives, and citrus fruits thrive in the hot temperatures, and these ingredients play a significant role in the cuisine of the South. Fresh, seasonal produce is a hallmark of Southern cooking, with dishes like Rocal Mediterranean Salad, made with tomatoes, cucumbers, and olives, highlighting the simplicity and freshness of the local ingredients. Olive oil, which is produced in abundance in the South, is used as both a cooking medium and a dressing, lending a rich, fruity flavor to many dishes. The Southern diet is also heavily influenced by seafood, with fresh fish, shellfish, and sea vegetables such as seaweed being essential components of the cuisine. Grilled fish, seafood

stews, and raw preparations like ceviche are staples in the South, where the coastal proximity allows for an abundance of marine life to be incorporated into meals.

The use of herbs and spices also varies significantly between the North and South. In the North, herbs like rosemary, thyme, and garlic are frequently used to season meats and stews, adding depth and warmth to the dishes. In the South, lighter, more aromatic herbs like basil, oregano, and parsley are used to complement the fresh vegetables and seafood, creating a bright, refreshing flavor profile. The influence of Mediterranean and Middle Eastern cuisines in the South is reflected in the frequent use of spices like cumin, coriander, and saffron, which are used to season rice, meat, and vegetable dishes.

Local ingredients in Rocal not only shape the flavors of the cuisine but also contribute to the way dishes are prepared and served. In the North, slow-cooking methods such as braising and stewing are common, as these techniques allow the tougher cuts of meat and root vegetables to become tender and flavorful. In the South, grilling and roasting are preferred methods, particularly for seafood and vegetables, which are cooked quickly to preserve their delicate flavors. The choice of cooking method is directly influenced by the ingredients available in each region, and these methods highlight the versatility of local produce and meats.

The importance of local ingredients in Rocal cuisine is further reflected in the growing movement toward sustainability and farm-to-table dining. As awareness of the environmental impact of food production increases, many chefs in Rocal are returning to their roots, using locally sourced, organic ingredients to create dishes that are both flavorful and environmentally responsible. By focusing on seasonal produce and ethically sourced meats, Rocal's chefs are ensuring that the culinary traditions of the region remain grounded in the principles of sustainability and respect for the land.

In conclusion, local ingredients are the foundation of Rocal's diverse culinary traditions, shaping regional dishes and influencing the way food is prepared and enjoyed. Whether it's the hearty meats and root vegetables of the North or the fresh seafood and vibrant vegetables of the South, Rocal's cuisine is a celebration of the land and its resources, offering a rich tapestry of flavors that reflect the diversity of the region.

Chapter 12
The Cultural Significance of Food in Rocal

Food in Rocal is not merely a means of sustenance; it is a powerful expression of the region's cultural identity, heritage, and traditions. It reflects the values, beliefs, and social dynamics that have shaped the lives of its people for centuries. The act of preparing, sharing, and enjoying food in Rocal is a deeply ingrained practice, woven into the fabric of daily life and communal interactions. From family meals to grand celebrations, food plays a central role in how the people of Rocal connect with each other, with their past, and with the land that sustains them.

The cultural significance of food in Rocal extends far beyond the kitchen, where it is often seen as a form of communication, a symbol of hospitality, and a means of honoring relationships. In Rocal society, the sharing of food is a way to build bonds, show respect, and demonstrate love and generosity. Whether it is a small family gathering or a grand feast, the act of offering food to others is seen as a gesture of goodwill and care. Meals are often prepared with great attention to detail, reflecting the effort and thought that goes into creating dishes that will nourish not just the body, but also the spirit.

Food also holds immense spiritual and ceremonial importance in Rocal culture. Many of the region's festivals, religious rituals, and community events are centered around food. Special dishes are prepared for religious holidays, weddings, and other significant occasions, each dish symbolizing a particular blessing or aspect of life. For example, during major religious festivals, elaborate meals are shared among family and friends, reinforcing the values of community, unity, and spiritual connection. The food served during these occasions often carries symbolic meanings, from the use of specific ingredients believed to bring good fortune to the preparation methods that evoke a sense of tradition and continuity.

The connection between food and cultural identity is also evident in Rocal's emphasis on local ingredients and culinary practices. The region's diverse landscapes—from fertile valleys to coastal shores—have shaped the flavors and dishes that define Rocal cuisine. Each region has its own unique culinary traditions, yet all are tied together by a deep respect for the land and its bounty. This reverence for nature is a key aspect of the cultural significance of food in Rocal, where meals are seen as a reflection of the earth's gifts and a celebration of its abundance.

In this chapter, we will explore how food in Rocal transcends its role as a mere necessity and becomes a vital part of the cultural and social fabric. By examining the ways in which food is intertwined with Rocal's traditions, rituals, and everyday life, we will gain a deeper understanding of how it shapes the identity and values of the region's people.

Food as a Reflection of Identity

In Rocal, food is far more than a practical necessity; it is a vital expression of identity, a window into the values, culture, and history of the people who call the region home. The culinary traditions of Rocal are deeply embedded in the daily lives of its inhabitants, reflecting a rich tapestry of influences that span generations. Rocal cuisine embodies the essence of its people—shaped by geography, history, and communal practices—each dish telling a story of its region, its agricultural heritage, and its evolving relationship with the world. Through food, the Rocal people express their pride in their heritage, their respect for tradition, and their ability to adapt to the changing times.

Rocal's cuisine is diverse and varies significantly from region to region, yet it shares a common thread that unites its people: a profound connection to the land and a deep reverence for locally sourced ingredients. The food traditions in Rocal serve as an anchor to the past, allowing people to connect with their roots, whether they are from the mountains, the plains, or the coastal regions. Local ingredients like native grains, vegetables, herbs, and meats form the foundation of Rocal dishes. Whether it is lamb stew in the north, grilled fish on the coast, or rich legumes in the plains, the food mirrors the landscape, making it an intrinsic part of the identity of the people who live there.

Beyond the ingredients and techniques, food in Rocal is symbolic of the values that define the culture. For instance, hospitality is a key pillar of Rocal society, and food is one of the most significant ways of expressing this hospitality. The act of inviting someone into one's home and sharing a meal is considered a mark of respect and generosity. The importance of food in this context is reflected in the large meals that are often shared with extended family, friends, and even strangers, emphasizing the value placed on community and togetherness. Whether served in grand banquets or simple family dinners, the food reflects an openness, a willingness to share, and an emphasis on connection.

Food also acts as a form of cultural storytelling. Recipes and cooking techniques are passed down through generations, serving as a bridge between the past and present. For example, Rocal Baklava, a sweet dessert made with filo pastry, nuts, and honey, has become synonymous with the region's hospitality and is often prepared for special occasions. It is not just a dish; it is a tradition, a piece of history that connects each generation to those that came before it. Through such culinary traditions, food becomes a language, speaking volumes about the values, customs, and history of the Rocal people.

Moreover, food in Rocal plays a significant role in shaping national and regional identities. In a country where different regions have their distinct flavors and cooking styles, food serves as a marker of identity and belonging. Northern Rocal, for example, is known for its hearty stews and meat-centric dishes, whereas the southern regions are celebrated for their seafood and lighter, vegetable-based dishes. These distinctions not only reflect the geography of the land but also the cultural identities of the people who inhabit these regions. The North's reliance on livestock and root vegetables versus the South's focus on fishing and farming creates a culinary map that mirrors the diversity and pride of Rocal's people.

In a modern, globalized world, Rocal's food traditions continue to evolve, yet the essence of the cuisine remains rooted in its cultural identity. Chefs and home cooks alike continue to innovate and experiment, combining traditional recipes with modern techniques, yet the spirit of Rocal food—the sense of connection, community, and history—remains unchanged. Food continues to be a mirror of Rocal's identity, a reflection of its values, and a celebration of its rich cultural heritage.

Celebrations and Rituals: The Role of Food in Rocal Traditions

In Rocal, food is at the heart of every celebration and ritual, underscoring its importance in marking life's most significant moments. Whether it's a religious holiday, a wedding, or a community festival, food plays a pivotal role in bringing people together, honoring cultural traditions, and symbolizing the blessings of life. Each celebration in Rocal is accompanied by a carefully prepared feast, with dishes that are rich in meaning, symbolism, and flavor. These meals reflect the region's deep connection to food as a communal, spiritual, and celebratory act.

Religious and cultural festivals in Rocal are often centered around food. For example, during major religious holidays like Eid al-Fitr, Eid al-Adha, and the Harvest Festival, families and communities come together to share elaborate meals. These festivals are an opportunity to honor the divine, give thanks for the abundance of the harvest, and strengthen social bonds. Special dishes that are not typically found in everyday meals are prepared to mark the occasion, making these dishes a symbolic part of the celebration. Rocal Lamb, stuffed with herbs and spices, for example, might be served during Eid as a symbol of abundance, sacrifice, and generosity.

In addition to religious holidays, Rocal weddings are grand affairs that also revolve around food. Food at a wedding is not merely sustenance; it is a celebration of life, love, and the joining of two families. A traditional wedding banquet in Rocal often includes multiple courses, each representing a different aspect of the couple's journey together. From appetizers made with freshly caught seafood to elaborate grilled meats and decadent desserts like Rocal Baklava or Date-stuffed Pastries, each dish is carefully chosen to represent prosperity, fertility, and joy. The wedding meal is an opportunity for family and friends to come together, share in the couple's happiness, and honor their union with the gift of food.

Beyond the religious and social holidays, food plays a central role in the everyday rituals of Rocal life. The concept of "breaking bread" together is a sacred one, representing unity and communion. Families often gather for weekly meals, where the sharing of food is symbolic of unity, respect, and love. The ritual of preparing meals as a family or community has been passed down through generations, where cooking becomes an expression of care, commitment, and connection. Traditional dishes like Rocal Stew or Vegetable Pilaf are often prepared in large quantities, symbolizing abundance and the desire to nourish those you love.

Food is also deeply tied to rites of passage. When a child reaches a certain age or celebrates a significant milestone, food is often used as a way of marking the event. For instance, the first birthday of a child in Rocal is often celebrated with a special feast, where traditional dishes like stuffed breads and fruit-based desserts are served. These meals, designed to nourish both body and soul, act as a reminder of the importance of food in shaping memories and traditions.

The role of food in Rocal rituals extends beyond human milestones—it is also present in honoring the land and the seasons. Seasonal festivals, like the Harvest Feast, celebrate the end of the growing season, where the fruits of the earth are harvested and enjoyed by communities. The preparation of these meals symbolizes gratitude for the land's abundance and the work of farmers and harvesters. Foods made from freshly harvested crops, like grilled corn, vegetable stews, and fruit compotes, are shared as a way to give thanks for the land's generosity and to celebrate the harvest.

In essence, the rituals and celebrations of Rocal revolve around the fundamental role that food plays in connecting people to their cultural heritage, their faith, and their communities. Whether it's a wedding, a religious festival, or a simple family gathering, food is woven into the very fabric of life's most important moments. It is a medium through which joy, gratitude, and unity are expressed, and its significance transcends its role as mere sustenance. Through food, Rocal traditions are kept alive, passed down to future generations, and celebrated in the most profound way possible.

How Rocal Food Brings People Together

Food in Rocal is more than just something to be eaten—it is a force that brings people together. The act of sharing food, whether in a family home, a local restaurant, or a large public festival, is a communal experience that reinforces the values of unity, hospitality, and connection. In a region as diverse as Rocal, where different cultures and traditions converge, food serves as a universal language that transcends individual backgrounds and fosters a sense of belonging.

At the heart of Rocal food culture is the concept of community. Rocal meals are almost always shared, and this communal approach to dining is central to the social fabric of the region. Whether it's a small family dinner, a neighborhood gathering, or a large-scale public celebration, food is the centerpiece that draws people together. The traditional family-style meal, where dishes are placed in the center of the table for everyone to share, reflects the Rocal belief that food is best enjoyed when shared with others. This communal style of dining encourages conversation, fosters a sense of intimacy, and allows for the exchange of stories, laughter, and memories.

The sharing of food in Rocal is not just about sustenance; it is an expression of generosity, hospitality, and love. Inviting someone to share a meal is a powerful gesture in Rocal culture, symbolizing respect and care. The Rocal people take great pride in hosting guests, ensuring that they are well-fed and comfortable. Meals are often prepared with great attention to detail, and hosts go out of their way to make their guests feel welcome, offering them the best dishes and ensuring that there is always enough food to go around. This emphasis on hospitality reflects the deep-seated belief in the importance of community and the social ties that bind people together.

Food also plays a pivotal role in fostering connections between different generations. In Rocal, it is common for family members of all ages to gather around the table for meals. Grandparents, parents, and children sit together, sharing not only food but also stories and traditions. The preparation of food is often a family affair, with multiple generations working together to create traditional dishes that have been passed down through the years. This shared cooking experience strengthens family bonds and ensures that cultural traditions are preserved for future generations.

In larger gatherings, such as weddings, religious holidays, or national festivals, food becomes a focal point for the community. These events often involve the preparation of massive quantities of food, which are shared by family, friends, and neighbors. The act of feeding a large group of people creates a sense of collective celebration and reinforces the idea of unity within the community. During these events, food is not just about nourishment—it is about honoring relationships, reinforcing cultural identity, and celebrating the bonds that connect people.

Rocal's food culture also extends beyond the home, bringing people together in public spaces. Local markets, food stalls, and outdoor festivals are vibrant hubs of social interaction, where people gather to enjoy traditional dishes, connect with others, and celebrate their cultural heritage. In these spaces, food acts as a catalyst for conversation and connection, allowing people from diverse backgrounds to come together over shared meals.

In a world that is increasingly fast-paced and fragmented, food in Rocal remains a constant source of unity and togetherness. It is a means by which people connect with their history, culture, and one another. Whether it's a small, intimate gathering or a large, communal feast, Rocal food brings people together in a way that transcends the boundaries of time, geography, and social class. Through food, the Rocal people share their stories, their values, and their love for one another, ensuring that the bonds of community and family remain strong for generations to come.

Conclusion

Rocal cuisine is not just a reflection of the region's agricultural bounty or its historical influences; it is a living, evolving expression of the identity and values of its people. The journey through Rocal's culinary world reveals a rich tapestry of flavors, techniques, and traditions, each connected to the land and the unique stories of the individuals who shape this vibrant culture. From the robust, hearty dishes of the northern mountains to the light, fresh offerings of the southern coast, every meal tells a story — of geography, history, community, and identity.

Food in Rocal is deeply intertwined with cultural practices, rituals, and social dynamics. It serves as a medium for expressing hospitality, a symbol of community, and a tool for honoring the past while embracing the future. The importance of food transcends its role as nourishment — it is a way to connect with others, celebrate life's milestones, and preserve cultural heritage. Whether it's a simple family meal, a festive gathering, or a religious holiday, food has the power to bring people together, foster connections, and reinforce shared values.

The fusion of ancient cooking methods with modern culinary innovations has allowed Rocal cuisine to remain dynamic, constantly adapting to new influences and trends while staying grounded in its cultural roots. As Rocal food continues to evolve, it reflects the region's ability to blend tradition with progress, keeping the essence of its culinary heritage intact while embracing global trends and technological advancements.

Rocal's diverse culinary traditions also highlight the region's respect for local ingredients and sustainable practices. As food culture worldwide shifts toward more sustainable, farm-to-table practices, Rocal's commitment to using fresh, locally sourced ingredients remains a key element of its culinary identity. This dedication ensures that Rocal's food culture remains relevant and continues to thrive, preserving its rich history while looking toward a future shaped by innovation, sustainability, and global influence.

A Taste of Rocal: Why You Should Try These Recipes

Rocal cuisine is an invitation to discover the heart and soul of a rich cultural heritage through its vibrant flavors, unique ingredients, and time-honored cooking techniques. From the first bite, Rocal dishes captivate the senses, offering a blend of tradition, innovation, and fresh ingredients that provide an unparalleled gastronomic experience. But beyond its taste, Rocal food represents something much deeper: a connection to the land, a reflection of centuries of culinary practices, and a celebration of the people who continue to shape its food culture.

One of the most compelling reasons to try Rocal recipes is the diversity of its culinary traditions. The variety of regional dishes in Rocal, shaped by the differing climates, landscapes, and cultural influences, ensures that there is something for every palate. Whether you're a fan of hearty, savory stews, fresh, vibrant salads, or sweet, indulgent desserts, Rocal cuisine has an array of dishes that will both delight and satisfy. The hearty Rocal Lamb Stew from the northern highlands, the fresh Grilled Fish from the coastal regions, and the sweet, syrupy Rocal Baklava are just a few examples of how Rocal cuisine captures a full spectrum of flavors—from the rich and comforting to the light and refreshing.

Rocal cuisine's emphasis on using fresh, local ingredients is another reason to explore its dishes. Whether you're savoring a salad made with locally grown tomatoes, or enjoying a fish dish prepared with freshly caught seafood, the flavors of the region's produce are unparalleled. The emphasis on seasonality means that Rocal recipes celebrate the natural bounty of the land, ensuring that every meal is a reflection of the freshest ingredients available at the time. Cooking with such vibrant, high-quality ingredients not only makes for delicious food but also fosters a deeper appreciation for the land and the labor that goes into growing and sourcing these ingredients.

Moreover, Rocal dishes offer an opportunity to connect with the region's cultural and historical roots. Many recipes have been passed down for generations, often originating from a time when food was grown, prepared, and shared within small, tight-knit communities. By trying Rocal recipes, you are not just enjoying a meal—you are participating in a long tradition that has been preserved and refined over centuries. These dishes are filled with stories and customs, offering a taste of history that can only be understood by experiencing it firsthand.

In addition to its deep cultural roots, Rocal cuisine is also an exciting area for innovation. Modern chefs in Rocal have begun experimenting with new cooking techniques and international influences while still honoring the region's culinary heritage. Whether through the fusion of traditional ingredients with contemporary cooking methods, or the incorporation of global culinary trends, Rocal food remains relevant and dynamic. These innovative twists provide an exciting opportunity to experience Rocal cuisine in new and creative ways, making the experience even more appealing to contemporary diners.

But beyond the food itself, trying Rocal recipes is an opportunity to connect with others. Food in Rocal is meant to be shared, whether at a family dinner table or a large public feast. By preparing and enjoying Rocal dishes with loved ones, you partake in the same social and cultural practices that have been central to the region's people for generations. Rocal cuisine is an experience of community, and it is through sharing these meals that you can truly understand the region's emphasis on togetherness and hospitality.

In conclusion, trying Rocal recipes is not just about tasting new and exciting food. It is about experiencing the culture, history, and values of Rocal, all while enjoying the fresh, vibrant flavors that make this cuisine so unique. Whether you are exploring traditional recipes passed down through generations or embracing modern twists on classic dishes, Rocal food offers an unforgettable culinary journey that will leave you both nourished and inspired.

Preserving the Tradition for Future Generations

The preservation of Rocal's culinary traditions is vital to maintaining the cultural heritage of the region. With the rise of globalization and the influence of modern cooking techniques, there is a risk that traditional practices may be lost or forgotten. However, in Rocal, the people have made it a priority to ensure that the culinary traditions that have shaped their culture are passed down to future generations. From the intricate preparation of traditional dishes to the preservation of locally sourced ingredients, every aspect of Rocal cuisine is deeply tied to the identity and history of its people. The challenge, then, is how to preserve this rich culinary heritage while embracing the inevitable changes that come with time and progress.

One key aspect of preserving Rocal's culinary traditions is the passing down of recipes and cooking techniques. In many households, cooking is an act of cultural transmission. Elders teach younger generations the secrets of preparing traditional dishes, passing along not only the recipes but also the skills, techniques, and cultural context behind each dish. These teachings are often done informally—through hands-on experience in the kitchen, as younger family members watch and participate in the cooking process. This method of learning ensures that the techniques are deeply ingrained, not just in the mind, but in the muscle memory of the cook. By engaging in this process, younger generations develop a deep respect for their culinary heritage and the value of preserving these traditions.

Another important aspect of preserving Rocal cuisine is the sustainable sourcing of ingredients. Many traditional Rocal dishes rely on locally grown produce, meats, and seafood, and these ingredients are a key component of what makes Rocal food so unique. As global demand for food grows, however, the methods of sourcing ingredients can change, sometimes at the expense of sustainability and local farming practices. To preserve the integrity of Rocal cuisine, it is crucial to support local farmers and fishermen who continue to produce the high-quality, seasonal ingredients that are integral to the region's culinary traditions. By promoting sustainable agriculture and responsible sourcing, Rocal can ensure that future generations have access to the fresh, flavorful ingredients that define their food culture.

Furthermore, education plays a vital role in the preservation of Rocal food traditions. Culinary schools, local food markets, and community initiatives are all working to educate younger generations about the importance of their culinary heritage. By introducing children and young adults to traditional Rocal recipes, cooking techniques, and the history behind the food, these institutions help to ensure that future generations understand the significance of their culinary traditions and feel a sense of pride in preserving them. This education also includes fostering an appreciation for regional ingredients, learning about the agricultural cycles, and respecting the processes that make Rocal food so special.

The role of food festivals, cooking competitions, and cultural events cannot be overstated in this effort to preserve Rocal's culinary traditions. These celebrations allow the community to come together to showcase their local dishes, promote traditional cooking methods, and celebrate the region's food culture. Events like Rocal Food Festivals and Heritage Cooking Competitions provide opportunities for both locals and visitors to experience Rocal's rich culinary diversity and help to keep the culture alive for future generations. These gatherings also provide a platform for chefs and home cooks to experiment with new ideas while staying true to the region's traditional flavors and techniques.

Finally, preserving the tradition of Rocal cuisine also involves embracing innovation without losing sight of the past. While it's essential to protect the authenticity of traditional recipes, there is room for creativity and evolution within the culinary tradition. The integration of modern cooking techniques, such as sous-vide cooking or molecular gastronomy, can be done in a way that enhances traditional dishes while maintaining their cultural integrity. By blending tradition with modernity, Rocal cuisine can continue to evolve while staying connected to its roots.

In conclusion, preserving the culinary traditions of Rocal for future generations is a multifaceted effort that involves passing down recipes and techniques, supporting sustainable sourcing, educating younger generations, and celebrating the culture through events and festivals. By making a collective effort to honor and preserve the culinary heritage of the region, Rocal can ensure that its food traditions continue to thrive, evolve, and inspire for years to come.

Cooking as a Cultural Expression

In Rocal, cooking is not just a skill; it is a powerful form of cultural expression. The way people prepare, cook, and share food reflects the values, beliefs, and social dynamics of the society. Food is an intimate part of everyday life in Rocal, providing a means of communication, celebration, and connection. It is through cooking that the people of Rocal express their creativity, respect for tradition, and love for community, making food a vital aspect of their cultural identity.

Cooking as a cultural expression in Rocal begins with the selection and preparation of ingredients. Every dish tells a story, and each ingredient has a purpose. The use of locally sourced, seasonal produce, meats, and spices is a way of honoring the land and the environment, recognizing the importance of the natural resources that sustain the region. In Rocal cuisine, food is a direct reflection of the relationship between the people and their land, and the preparation of meals is a sacred act that connects individuals to the earth and to one another. When preparing a traditional dish, such as a Rocal Lamb Stew or Seafood Paella, the cook honors the centuries of knowledge passed down through generations, each layer of flavor and technique representing the legacy of those who came before them.

The presentation of food in Rocal also plays a key role in how cooking is used as a cultural expression. A beautifully prepared dish is not just about aesthetics; it's about creating an experience that honors both the ingredients and the people sharing the meal. The art of plating, garnishing, and serving is as much about conveying respect and care as it is about creating an enjoyable sensory experience. In Rocal, meals are often served family-style, with large platters placed in the center of the table for everyone to share. This communal way of dining reflects the importance of togetherness and unity, where food becomes a symbol of generosity, hospitality, and the bonds of community.

Cooking also serves as a means of storytelling. The origins of a dish, the way it is prepared, and the reasons behind certain cooking practices all carry meaning that connects the present generation to its cultural roots. Food becomes a way of remembering history, celebrating milestones, and passing down traditions. Each dish represents a chapter of the region's story, with ingredients, techniques, and customs that have been honed over time. From family recipes passed down through generations to the resurgence of forgotten dishes, cooking in Rocal serves as a form of cultural preservation, allowing the people to express their collective identity and heritage through food.

Moreover, cooking in Rocal is a communal activity that fosters relationships and strengthens social bonds

The act of preparing food together is a form of collaboration and connection, and meals are an opportunity for people to gather, celebrate, and share their lives. Food brings people together across social, economic, and cultural divides, providing a common ground where differences can be bridged and shared experiences can be celebrated.

In conclusion, cooking in Rocal is more than just a practical activity—it is a form of cultural expression that connects people to their past, their land, and each other. Through the preparation, presentation, and sharing of food, Rocal's culinary traditions remain a vital part of the region's identity, a means of expressing creativity, honoring tradition, and fostering community. Food in Rocal is a celebration of culture, a language that transcends words, and a powerful symbol of the region's values and heritage.

www.ingramcontent.com/pod-product-compliance
Lightning Source LLC
LaVergne TN
LVHW061556070526
838199LV00077B/7077